The Political Economy of Robert Lowe

The Political Economy of Robert Lowe

John Maloney

palgrave
macmillan

First published 2005 by
PALGRAVE MACMILLAN
Houndmills, Basingstoke, Hampshire RG21 6XS and
175 Fifth Avenue, New York, N.Y. 10010
Companies and representatives throughout the world

PALGRAVE MACMILLAN is the global academic imprint of the Palgrave Macmillan division of St. Martin's Press, LLC and of Palgrave Macmillan Ltd. Macmillan® is a registered trademark in the United States, United Kingdom and other countries. Palgrave is a registered trademark in the European Union and other countries.

ISBN 1–4039–4782–1 hardback

This book is printed on paper suitable for recycling and made from fully managed and sustained forest sources.

A catalogue record for this book is available from the British Library.

Library of Congress Cataloging-in-Publication Data
Maloney, John, 1948–
The political economy of Robert Lowe / by John Maloney.
p. cm.
Includes bibliographical references and index.
ISBN 1–4039–4782–1 (hardback)
1. Sherbrooke, Robert Lowe, Viscount, 1811–1892. 2. Economists—Great Britain—Biography. I. Title.

HB103.S54A3 2005
330.15'3'092—dc22

2004051338

10 9 8 7 6 5 4 3 2 1
14 13 12 11 10 09 08 07 06 05

Printed and bound in Great Britain by
Antony Rowe Ltd, Chippenham and Eastbourne

For Mary and Roger

Contents

Acknowledgements

I would like to thank Professor Mark Blaug, the late Dr Fred Meyer, Dr Pedro Teixeira, Mr Allan Ward, Professor Donald Winch and Mr Michael Wright, all of whom read and commented on the first draft of this book. I would also like to thank the staff of the National Archive at Kew, the British Library, the Bodleian Library and the House of Lords Library for their help; also Professor Steve Medema, editor, and the History of Economics Society for permission to reproduce material which originally appeared in the *Journal of the History of Economic Thought*. Most authorship has its moments of boredom or down-heartedness but this book was pure pleasure to write from start to finish. The greatest thanks of all must therefore go to Robert Lowe, Viscount Sherbrooke.

Chronology

1811 born at Bingham, Nottinghamshire
1842 goes to New South Wales
1843 becomes member of the legislative council of New South Wales
1850 returns to England
1851 becomes leader-writer for *The Times*
1852 elected Liberal MP for Kidderminster
1853 joint secretary of the Board of Control for India
1855 vice-president of the Board of Trade
1858 in opposition
1859 elected Liberal MP for Calne; becomes vice-president of the Board of Education
1864 returns to government backbenches
1866 in opposition
1868 resigns from *The Times*
1868 elected Liberal MP for London University; becomes Chancellor of the Exchequer
1873 home secretary
1874 returns to opposition backbenches
1880 goes to House of Lords as Viscount Sherbrooke
1892 dies at Caterham, Surrey.

1
Go Out and Govern New South Wales

Arriving in Downing Street brings out the essence of many a politician, but the two most famous reactions are from the same year. In February 1868 Disraeli announced he had climbed to the top of the greasy pole. He and his minority government were not there long, and in December it was Gladstone's turn to declare that his mission was to pacify Ireland.

But another Liberal, sent by Gladstone that same month to 11 Downing Street, reacted unexpectedly. Not in breaking into verse, for he had been a poet from his schooldays. But Robert Lowe called his poem 'Success' and the word was charged with pathos. 'Success has come but ah! has come too late', he mourned.

> O vanity of vanities! For Truth
> And Time dry up the spring where joy was rife
> Teach us we are but shadows of our youth
> And mock us with the emptiness of life.[1]

At 57, Lowe felt his promotion to the cabinet had come too late for him to enjoy it to the full. But the other striking thing about his reaction to being made Chancellor of the Exchequer was his lack of surprise. In this he was almost alone. It was not just that he was a maverick figure who had made much of his reputation – both as politician and leader-writer on *The Times* – by attacking Gladstone. His positive qualifications for the job also seemed slender. No one doubted his command of economics. But, then as now, no one saw this as the first requirement for a successful Chancellor. The distinct and more relevant field of finance was one he had never cultivated much. There is no reason to find false modesty (never a Lowe quality anyway) in his words to his brother 'Dear Henry, I am Chancellor of the Exchequer with everything to learn.'[2]

Going to the Treasury forced Lowe to clarify and defend many of his opinions, as will be seen. But he could hardly occupy a more combative position in the front line of political economy than he was already doing. In 1862, as vice-president of the Board of Education, he had subjected schools to payment by examination results. Since then he had mounted a furious attack on the trade unions, and clashed with John Stuart Mill over the Irish question and the place of political economy within it. He had opposed the bulk of his own party, earned the enmity of younger Liberals, and made some of the greatest parliamentary speeches of the Victorian age in his opposition to the doubling of the franchise in the 1867 Reform Bill. Informing all these episodes was an economic perspective that he believed had been handed down to him from Adam Smith. His preoccupations as Chancellor, far from pushing him blinking into the limelight as an economist, displaced other roles he might have played on the economic battleground. It is not taking much of a risk to guess that loyalty to the classical school in its decline would have been one of them.

For between 1868 and 1873, the years of Lowe's Chancellorship, English classical economics fell apart. First W.T. Thornton demolished one of its main pillars, the theory of the wage fund. This was the idea of a fund, fixed at any one time, which had to be paid out to support labour before it could produce goods and services. Because it was fixed, workers could gain only at each others' expense. Its demise thus opened up possibilities for redistribution and effective trade unionism that classical economics had kept more or less closed. The question now was how Mill would respond, and the answer was immediate. In a startling recantation, Mill pronounced Thornton right and the theory wrong. Then in 1871 W.S. Jevons' *Theory of Political Economy* announced the start of the neoclassical era and the end of Ricardo's attempt to shunt economics onto a 'wrong-headed' line. Value, the most fundamental concept in economics, was proclaimed a subjective phenomenon, based on the utility of a good to the person who owned it. The labour theory of value was taken off for burial, though it was the next generation of economists who would try to bury Karl Marx. In the same year as Jevons' *Theory*, Cliffe Leslie launched his main assault on deductive economics, calling for the classical edifice to be levelled to the ground and replaced by an economics built on historical evidence, not on stereotypes of impossibly greedy individuals. In this last demand he was joined by John Ruskin, whose anti-economic invective reached its apotheosis in *Fors Clavigera*. Half-hearted attempts by Mill and J.E. Cairnes to save the classical tradition ended with their deaths in 1873 and 1875.

But the crisis passed Lowe by. He was too busy. Even in the 1860s, Chancellor of the Exchequer was a full-time job for anyone but Gladstone himself. And for Lowe the Chancellorship brought about a more immediate and personal crisis.

Lowe's problem was that he was *not* a straightforwardly conservative economist with a closed mind, as critics in his lifetime and more recently have depicted him. Indeed he stands out as a particularly vivid example of a Benthamite coming to terms with the increased power of the nineteenth-century state. The coming to terms, however, had mostly been at Lowe's own idiosyncratic speed. When he acceded to the Treasury, time ran out for Lowe. The changing mid-Victorian state and the gradual switch from indirect to direct taxation were issues on which he must take an immediate position.

Lowe was the most accomplished economist to inhabit 11 Downing Street in the nineteenth century, though, if anachronism and league tables are to be allowed, he would rank below Dalton and no higher than Gaitskell. The other records he set were less happy ones: the only Chancellor to have his skull fractured at an election meeting, or to be challenged to two duels, or to take refuge from demonstrators underneath the palace of Westminster, or to have to withdraw his entire budget.[3]

All these achievements are clues to a contentious character. Lowe was a hard, fierce man with a gift for enmity. Disraeli designated him the one man in London whose hand he would refuse to shake. Victoria vastly preferred even Gladstone. In Lowe's fragment of autobiography he explains 'With a quiet temper and a real wish to please, I have been obliged to submit all my life to an unpopularity which I really did not deserve.'[4] It is unlikely this assessment convinced anyone else.

Innocent parties would be drawn into Lowe's love of a good fight. Arriving early with Lowe at their joint destination, the Lord Chancellor of the day was taken aback to hear Lowe suggest filling the time by starting an argument with the cabman about the fare. But travelling with Lowe was often a hazardous business. As an undergraduate he went journeying through the Highlands with Wordsworth (whose son was Lowe's friend) and decided to torment the old man with non-stop praise of Walter Scott. The incident is gleefully recounted in Lowe's autobiography, 40 years later.

No one weighed up whether the frequent charm of Lowe's company was worth such incidents because no one was neutral enough to cite both the incidents and the charm – a significant detail in itself. But Sir George Cornewall Lewis, one of Lowe's predecessors at the Exchequer and his closest political friend until his death in 1863, said he would rather be cast away on a desert island with Lowe than with anyone else. Lord Chief Justice Cockburn said the same thing, although sensibly substituting a country house on a wet day for the desert island.[5] Unlike many brilliant talkers, Lowe was an excellent listener, which – added to Lowe's own preferences in the matter – may help explain why most of his close friends were women. And Goschen, far from being a sentimentalist, spoke of Lowe's 'extreme kindness of heart', though the only evidence he adduced, the partiality to Lowe of children and pet animals, may carry less conclusive weight in a more cynical age.[6]

The more difficult side of Lowe's temperament may have owed something to his disability. He was born in 1811 into the happy and prosperous family of the rector of Bingham, Nottinghamshire. But he had the misfortune to be born an albino. Bright light was both necessary for clear vision and at the same time unbearable. Sitting in a good light with his eyes screwed up to avoid most of it was the tortured compromise forced upon this passionate reader.

For all his reserves of stoicism and determination, Lowe's condition dogged his education. His failure to get a first in mathematics at Oxford (he succeeded in classics) was a heavy blow. It can be attributed convincingly to his poor sight though one might discount a fellow-undergraduate's diagnosis that Lowe was so near-sighted that he rubbed out most of his work with his nose.[7] Still, a first in classics – and a first-class debating reputation at the Oxford Union – was not a bad springboard for the next leap.

But to where? A college fellowship was much harder to come by without ordination, a course Lowe firmly refused. In the end he only had to wait a year for a lay fellowship at Magdalen College. But the following year, 1836, he was surrendering it. Married men might not be fellows, and Lowe put marriage first. Instead he knuckled down to the drudgery of private tutoring. An application for the Chair of Greek at the University of Glasgow narrowly failed, and in 1840 Lowe left Oxford to read for the Bar.

He qualified in 1842, but his efforts had impaired his eyesight still further. His response was the move that inaugurated the political economy of Robert Lowe.

II

Lowe decided to go to New South Wales. In the first place, he needed to earn a large sum in a short while, given that blindness might truncate his working life at any time. The Australian Bar, he rightly surmised, was a place to make one's way quickly. But secondly his doctor pressed Australia on him as the only place where his sight might survive. Recommending the glaring sunshine of New South Wales sounds almost incredible – Lowe himself wondered if the doctor's judgement were absolutely reliable. But in 1842 he and his wife set sail, to receive a lavish welcome and prolonged hospitality from the Governor of New South Wales, Sir George Gipps. The friendship, as will be seen, was not to last.

Before it ended, however, Lowe was dealt another blow. Now his Australian doctor, William Bland, pronounced that blindness was imminent anyway unless he stopped work. Again Lowe doubted. Again he obeyed. When, driven by need, boredom and scepticism, he discarded Bland's warnings and resumed practice, his sight remained exactly the same. Lowe never forgave Bland and had a belated revenge in 1849 when the latter was nominated to the Senate of the proposed University of Sydney. Lowe crashed through the ultimate political and social taboo by reminding everyone that Bland was a former convict.

Most people were offended but few were surprised. Lowe had been attracting notoriety – or vice versa – ever since he had arrived in 1842. 'If he noticed that flames were crackling around him he reached out and fanned them' is Winter's (1976) comment on his career as a whole.[8] If so, the Australian years were the ones when he reached for the kerosene. His sojourn even included two challenges to duels. One was avoided when his opponent was arrested on the way to meet him, the other declined by Lowe on the grounds that his opponent, though now an alderman, had previously been a non-commissioned officer.

Lowe's political allegiances in New South Wales fell into three periods: the protégé of Governor Gipps, the champion of the squatters (graziers on Crown lands) against the Governor and the champion of almost everyone else against the squatters. However his Australian years may have prefigured his English political career – and the ways were many, as we shall see – an experience he never had to repeat in England was that of abuse and ridicule as an unprincipled political weathercock. Lowe, then as later better at handing out invective than receiving it, was deeply stung by this charge and believed, with undoubted sincerity, it to be wholly unfair. It was, at any rate, an accusation he never courted again.

Lowe arrived in New South Wales just as the colony was taking its first steps towards democracy. The old Legislative Council, its members nominated from London, was about to give way to a body of 24 elected members and 12 appointed by the Governor. Its taxing and spending powers, however, were severely limited; in particular, the crown was to retain all revenue from public lands.

It was the consequences of this restriction that drove Lowe and Gipps apart. Within a few months of Lowe's arrival in Australia the Governor had nominated him to the new council. But early in 1844, Gipps' straitened predicament was exacerbated as the Colonial Office sent five thousand new immigrants to New South Wales, to be assisted by a bounty out of the colonists' taxes. Gipps announced that the only way to raise the money was to tax the squatters. Lowe broke loose, re-positioned himself as the squatters' champion, resigned his nominated seat on the Council and stood for election as member for St Vincent and Auckland. The campaign was rough even by the standards of mid-nineteenth-century Australia, so much so that Lowe wrote to the *Sydney Morning Herald*, helpfully pointing out a few areas of opprobrium they had missed.

> I ride a very ugly horse, that clearly proves me as a theist, for who else could be so insensible to the beauties of the noblest animal of

> creation. I live in a very small house, which clearly shows I must have a contracted mind, and I am sometimes known to play at billiards, which shows a strong though, it may perhaps be expedient in candour to admit, not quite fully developed propensity for gambling.[9]

The reference to theism arose from recent attacks on Lowe after he had tried to save a client by arguing that he had been unable to prevent himself committing murder, as anyone acquainted with the new science of phrenology could demonstrate by examining the shape of his head. This was seen as more blasphemous than desperate, and the publicity continued when, after his client's execution, Lowe and his wife adopted the two children of the murder victim – a precedent never widely followed among defence counsel.

But by the time Lowe finally got elected, he was already moving away politically from the squatters. The crucial issue was the price of land. In 1842 this had been raised to £1 per acre, first to discourage people from buying land who lacked the resources to develop it efficiently, and second to raise money to assist the passage of poor emigrants. Lowe had opposed this fixed minimum price almost from the start – certainly once a downturn in 1843 left few buyers able to afford it. Now he increasingly saw it as a brake on modern farming and an unjust imposition on those who wanted to practise it. As long as the price remained high, few people would buy much of the land, so that the squatters would remain, grazing their sheep by grace of the Colonial Office and thus permanently in hock to London. Political independence as well as economic progress was thus being put on hold. 'Man is to be penned within narrow limits, that sheep and cattle may have room to roam at large.'[10]

But the worst was yet to come. In 1847, a proposed Land Bill from London ruled the squatters' privileges not excessive but insufficient. Now any squatter who wished to buy Crown lands at £1 an acre was to have a prescriptive right to do so. All competition was to be excluded. Earl Grey, Colonial Secretary and author of the new measure, explained that it was needed to prevent 'dispersion of the people', a precondition of a 'return to barbarism'.[11] Lowe asked how the free-trading Grey could consistently try to prevent freedom of movement, a mission which would in any case fail once Australians had made up their mind to 'disperse'. Concentration, he told the

Council, was the result, not the source of wealth: it was the 'natural tendency of human nature' for wealthy communities to concentrate. Until wealth was acquired it was equally natural for men to disperse and seek wealth where they thought they could find it.[12] Lowe's speech removed any last doubts about his oratorical powers, but the assembly was determined to back a Land Bill which Grey was determined to enact anyway. Undaunted, Lowe had the whole squatter question referred to a committee. He then managed to get control of it and write its report, in which he castigated the British government for repudiating the doctrine of supply and demand. 'The mind is astonished by the anomalous spectacle of a colony active, enterprising and energetic in all things, except the one alone for which it was founded – colonisation.'[13]

By now Lowe was immensely popular with much of the urban middle and working classes. Prevailed upon to desert St Vincent and stand for Sydney, he refused to seek the seat but said they could draft him if they liked. When they did, he used the hustings to protest his consistency throughout his pro- and anti-squatter phases.

> When I first made common cause with the squatters, they were an oppressed class, crushed by the heels of a despotic and arbitrary government, who sought to do what no government had a right to do, to tax them without their being represented... Since that period the times have changed – the circumstances have changed – and the squatters have changed, but I have not changed... I have been consistent in fighting for liberty – the squatters have been consistent in fighting for money.[14]

One subject on which Lowe did admit a change of mind was the transportation of convicts, which had temporarily ceased. Initially he supported its renewal as a source of cheap labour, but when in 1849 convicts began to arrive again, he supported the massive protest which resulted. Now cheap labour was to be deplored as keeping the squatters in their privileged position. Cut off the supply of convicts, and 'the large proprietor can no longer maintain his vast establishments. The landed aristocracy of the colony – the holders of princely domains – will sink overwhelmed by their own greatness.'[15] The Sydney working class, fearful of the new competition, were most hostile of all to renewed transportation. Yet the issue did not significantly add to Lowe's popularity with them. For one thing, he seemed untypically half-hearted about it. The rhetoric might be there, but there were incidents like the time he was due to chair a protest meeting and never bothered to turn up. But what really lost Lowe his working-class support, indeed turned it into equally violent enmity, was his view about public works.

The years 1848 and 1849 were bad for the workers not just because of the convict threat. Other forms of immigration were on the rise again, just as the economy and employment were turning down. A meeting was convened to demand public works for the unemployed. Lowe was invited to attend. Instead he sent them the following reply:

> Sir – I must beg to decline to attend your meeting for the following reasons:
>
> Because the revenue (which is principally raised from the wages of the people) ought to be expended for the good of all, and not just a particular class.
>
> Because it is just as improper to spend public money to keep up wages as to keep up rents or profits.
>
> Because I do not think the mechanics of Sydney ought to put themselves in the position of paupers receiving charitable relief at the expense of their equally distressed fellow-colonists.
>
> Because those who anticipated an immediate profit from the intended expenditure are the worst possible judges of its necessity.
>
> Because the attempt to prevent labour finding its level must, in my opinion, be useless or mischievous.
>
> Because I will never be a party to spending public money in order artificially to raise the price which employers of mechanics in the interior must pay for their services and thus to arrest the progress of improvement throughout the colony.[16]

It will be one of the themes of this book that Lowe was less inflexible than his doctrinaire reputation, in his lifetime and since, suggests. But the missive just quoted could hardly be bettered as a summary of the economic attitudes on which he was never to compromise. It was read out – twice, at popular request – to a meeting which, in the words of Martin (1893), was 'fairly aghast'. An Irishman bellowed some prefiguratory Keynesianism which would have been as alien to Lowe as his own sentiments were to the crowd.

> You have been termed paupers! And that by the pet of the people! ... In the name of God! (yelled the exasperated Mr Lynch) what does he mean? If the money was given by the Council to the mechanics, would they keep it buttoned up in their pockets? Would it not every Saturday be expended with a small shop-keeper, from whom it would travel on to the middleman and the merchant?[17]

III

All the while in Australia, Lowe had been chasing the day when he could return to England and feel secure about money. Now, in 1850, he decided that it had arrived. (He was right: the property he had bought in and around Sydney would be his main source of income for the rest of his life.) He was impatient to be gone. Parliament beckoned. Men he had known at Oxford had been members for years. Some had already been ministers. With few friends left in Australia, he slipped away with no kind of official farewell, though the public auction of his furniture was a popular sporting event which, unlike most episodes in Lowe's career, drew all classes together. But he did take with him the political experience which, he maintained ever after, was an invaluable practice and preparation for his career in England. His oratory had matured, so that members would sit up sharply for a Lowe speech right from his election for Kidderminster in 1852. He had also rehearsed most of the great themes which would define his political maturity. His monetary orthodoxy stepped into the light when a fellow Councillor proposed the government start lending banknotes on the security of landed property. Asked to join a committee to look at the 1841 Colonial Insolvency Act, he pronounced imprisonment for debt to be 'a practice from which human nature recoils with horror' and 'the foulest stain which yet disgraces the community'.[18] In his old age he would go all the way to the abolition of bankruptcy courts. Free trade was an early preoccupation – speaking against a tariff on grain in 1843, Lowe begged his colleagues not to make New South Wales 'an asylum for the exploded fallacies of the rest of the world'.[19] And running as a common thread through all his policy proposals was the Benthamism in which he never wavered. A parliamentary representative, he told the Sydney mob while it was still on his side, should pursue steadily 'the one great and high ultimatum of all government and all legislation, the greatest happiness of the greatest number'.[20]

2
The Limits to *Laissez-Faire*

It was free trade, however, that Lowe carried closest to his heart as he returned to England. The repeal of the Corn Laws, he wrote soon after he arrived home, 'overleaps the ordinary achievements of legislation as the Arc de Triomphe towers over the low-lying buildings at its feet'.[1] In one of his first parliamentary speeches he praised Gladstone's budget of 1853 for upholding 'the grand principle of Free Trade – far more valuable than Free Trade itself – that no one class in the country should be made tributary to another class'.[2]

Out-and-out protectionists might expose their economic ignorance, but to pick the finest flower of this ignorance, to savour the quintessence of muddle, it was necessary to visit 'strategic' trade theorists, advocates of commercial treaties or anyone with 'retaliation' in their vocabulary. Lowe knew his Ricardo. Abolishing tariffs – provided they were not needed to raise revenue – was an economic good whatever the other side did. Even to contemplate treaties which made free trade a multilateral, negotiated affair was to send out an economically illiterate message and fix surviving protectionists in their delusions.

So when in 1857 Lowe, now vice-president of the Board of Trade, sang his department's praises in a Commons debate, no one was surprised when he singled it out as 'the main agent in establishing those principles which rendered reciprocity treaties obsolete and unnecessary'. As 'the grave of protection and the cradle of free trade' it had performed an educational role as well as a directly administrative one.[3] The context of Lowe's speech was a motion to hold an inquiry into possible changes to the Board of Trade. The Board's critics, Lowe asserted, were mainly special interest groups who had rightly suffered from the Board's defence of the public interest. And, second only to its promotion of free trade, it had blessed the public with the principle of limited liability.

Here Lowe was speaking of an achievement in which he himself had partaken. His first main task at the Board had been to introduce the Joint Stock Companies Act of 1856. This measure not only cut the number of shareholders allowed to register as a limited-liability company from 25 to 7; it almost entirely swept away the Board's own role in investigating and regulating such firms.

It was not in the government's power, Lowe told parliament, to abort fraudulent companies. The effect of the current regulations was 'to embarrass, perhaps, a hundred honest, sound, *bona fide* concerns, in the vain and futile effort to correct the hundred-and-first'.[4] Indeed the main effect of the law's failed paternalism was to 'lull to sleep' the vigilance of individuals dealing with these companies. Now, instead, *caveat emptor* was to rule. A company need only proclaim publicly that liability was limited, and people, thus warned, could choose whether to do business with it.

The Bill also swept away (the railway companies excepted) the rule that 20 per cent of the capital subscribed towards a new company must be paid up at the start. Quite right too, said Lowe – all that had been required was a *declaration* that the company met the conditions. No one ever checked so that, once again, frauds and liars gained an advantage over honest men. Anyway, if you insisted on excessive paid-up capital, long before the firm could actually do anything with it, this was a standing temptation to dishonest directors to find a way to steal it. As for the proposal made in the House to fix a minimum price per share, 'can we imagine a more impolitic law than that which permits associations to be formed by the rich, but denies them to the poor?'[5]

In Lowe's peroration, he lifted the House's eyes from the technicalities of company law to the glories of political economy. After inviting it to find a single government in the history of the world which had erred on the side of giving too much freedom of commerce, he wound up with a characteristic definition of *laissez-faire* and description of the invisible hand:

> When the political economists say '*Laissez-faire*', they do not mean to say 'Leave all matters to blind chance; let everything go as it

> may.' What they mean by 'laissez faire' is, that we are not to interfere with human laws where other laws so much wiser exist. Man, Sir, with his free will, his caprices, and his errors, is as much under the rule and government of a natural law as the planet in its orbit, or as water, which always seeks its level. Those laws, planted by Infinite Sagacity, have the power of correcting and compensating errors... dearness producing cheapness and cheapness dearness; and thus the great machine of society is constantly kept oscillating to its centre... Who could have imagined it possible that a state of society resting on the most unlimited and unfettered liberty of action... would tend more to the prosperity and happiness of man than the most matured decrees of senates and of States? These are the wonders of the science of political economy...[6]

It was a memorable and much-praised speech, but the Act itself did little to justify Lowe's hopes that it would now be easier to start a business on limited capital. The trend towards concentration continued, though Lowe may well have believed that without it things would have been worse. And the Act's intended partner, a bill to extend limited liability in the case of partnerships, perished in the Commons despite more passionate advocacy from Lowe.[7] But in 1866 the issue erupted again when the Liberal government (of which Lowe was not a member) sought to strengthen both the limited-liability principle and its promise of popular capitalism, by allowing limited companies to issue shares in lower denominations than before. Lord Overstone led the attack, prompting Lowe to explain in *The Times* that

> The one fault that has never been forgiven by Lord Overstone is that it allows a number of comparatively poor men by combining their funds to compete on terms of equality with the single great capitalist... such men as Lord Overstone... regard society as mainly constituted for the purpose of enabling a few persons to make a great deal of money.[8]

Overstone had worried that cheap shares would mean working-class investors. Much government interference would then be required to protect these people from their own folly. This was well calculated to arouse Lowe. Sarcastically, he asked that, if the state were so much wiser than the people, should there not be 'a public officer without whose advice no person should be allowed to invest his own money?' Opposition to limited liability, he concluded, was 'in contradiction of the well-established principles of political economy, which prescribe that contracts ought to be free'.[9] Overstone and his allies wanted to prohibit limited-liability contracts even when both sides wanted them.

But this is to leap ahead. In the ten years between the 1856 Act and Lowe's backbench assault on Overstone, he had finished his term at the Board of Trade, served for five years as vice-president of the Board of Education, covered many economic issues in his leaders for *The Times*, suffered a fractured skull at an election riot in Kidderminster and retreated to the safer (politically – no one was less in need of physical courage) pasture of Calne in Wiltshire. We must retrace.

One of the Board of Trade's responsibilities was to regulate – or rather decide if it wished to regulate – the railways. In this way Lowe became involved in a subject on which it was characteristic for most politicians to be uncharacteristic. Gladstone had proposed railway nationalisation in 1844, and would circulate a similar proposal, but limited to Irish railways and fiercely opposed by Lowe himself, in 1872. One of Lowe's objections, presciently, concerned the odium which would befall the government as soon as anyone died in a nationalised accident. And this was only a reflection of the views he had submitted to a committee of inquiry into rail accidents, soon after leaving office on Palmerston's defeat in 1858.

Lowe started by telling the committee that public regulation of safety standards would increase the number of accidents as railway companies, secure in the knowledge that someone else was supposedly looking after their safety, relaxed their grip. A puzzled chairman tried to hold Lowe to the strict economics of the matter. Surely the *cost* to the company of the accident would be unchanged and so, therefore, would be its efforts to avoid one? Yes, said Lowe, but assuming regulation included speed limits, they would feel there was less risk of an accident. Well there would be, wouldn't there? said the chairman. Yes, admitted Lowe. And if a regulator ensured the track was properly maintained, you could surely have fewer accidents even without a reduction in speed? Yes, said Lowe, but what if the company's accounts were such that they would rather risk accidents than any further financial pressure? The chairman now began to grow a little warmer. Should the first object be the safety of the public or the pockets of the companies? 'I think it is too late to raise that question' was Lowe's imperturbable reply: 'we have given the preference to the commercial element in the matter, and we must take it and work it out as well as we can'. 'Without reference to life and limb?' 'Yes, we had our choice... it may or it may not be as good as the other plan, but... the mixture of the two systems will never work... you must take one or the other.' Lowe defended this by returning to his assertion that government regulation displaced a greater volume of private care. He threw in a proto-Hayekian line about how the State, once involved, would be on an irreversible path to complete control; then raised the spectre of railway companies bribing officials to find safety faults in their rivals' equipment. Another member now took over the questioning. Surely Mr Lowe would at least accept the need for someone to coordinate different companies' signalling codes? Drivers commonly had to cope with several different systems in the course of one journey. This, said Lowe, was undesirable, but not so undesirable as to make it advisable to remedy it: 'I would leave the companies to the penalties of the Law.'[10]

In thus putting purity of doctrine well above even logic, Lowe not only struck out against the fashion of being unwontedly statist when the railways came up for discussion, but also served up a feast which his critics (Mill 1868; Leslie 1879; Moore 1996) have so far left untasted. The one issue which barely came up was the question of regulating competition between the railways. When Lowe addressed the topic a few months later in a *Times* leader, he not only defended the railways' right to found a price cartel but, very surprisingly, called on parliament to make it legally binding. He 'sincerely rejoiced', he said, that the 21 largest companies had met to fix their fares 'so as to yield the largest amount of profit, reference being had to the interest of the public', whatever that means.[11]

The Liberals were out of office for a mere 18 months. In 1859, Palmerston was back and appointed Lowe vice-president of the Board of Education. His attempts to bring the ideas of Adam Smith into schools and universities – and his radical change of direction when a trebling of the electorate made it urgent to educate 'our new masters' – will be described in Chapter 4. But the vice-president's responsibilities included public health as well as education and here Lowe set off, instantly and with certitude, in a statist direction to which neither he nor public health was accustomed. In bringing in compulsory vaccination and the prosecution of objectors at Poor Law Guardians' expense, he drew on the *Wealth of Nations'* account of public goods as pretexts for state intervention. It is likely that, for once, Smith was convenient and not inspirational. One of Lowe's best qualities was his open-mindeness to the ideas of expert and determined administrators. Dogmas of which no politician could divest him would be put up for examination when civil servants invited him to join a public crusade.

Because they were occasional, Lowe savoured his own holidays from *laissez-faire*. 'Sheridan', he once explained to his civil servants, 'when he saw a highlander in a very large pair of trousers said that converts were always enthusiastic'.[12] There was to be no general conversion for Lowe, but over the years he found a good few exceptions to his principles. These exceptions were best handled by Liberals because, in James Winter's words, 'they alone understood why they were departing from a general principle and therefore could be trusted not to confuse the exception with the rule'.[13]

How far were the departures from principle occasioned by a still more general principle – utilitarianism? Entirely is the answer; Lowe never wavered from the view that utility be the sole ground in choosing between intervention and *laissez-faire*. This is not an empty statement; by no means all reformers took this view, and few as explicitly and doggedly as Lowe. But neither is it a statement of more than limited usefulness. The ethical goal of the greatest happiness of the greatest number yields few, if any, direct policy prescriptions. In practice all utilitarians have had to build a transmission mechanism before the felicific engine can turn the legislative wheels; and in practice this transmission mechanism has turned out to be a replacement for, not an appendage to, the engine. If Lowe's auxiliary principle is to be defined as '*laissez-faire* but...', we are simply back where we began, trying to systematise the 'but'. This is better attempted when the whole, lifelong, range of Lowe's policy stances has been considered.

3
Trade and Treaties

The theory of comparative advantage had shown that any two nations could gain by freeing up their trade with each other. The theory was seldom cited in political debate and, on its rare appearances in the Corn Laws controversy, contrived to look like a complicated irrelevance.[1] No one disputed that Britain had an *absolute* advantage in manufacturing and disadvantage in corn. Still, the theory was there to be drawn on when needed, and provided a framework for discussing the more contentious question of whether a nation should drop its tariffs even against a rival who refused to reciprocate.

Dogmatic free traders had no problem with this question: Bastiat compared a retaliatory tariff to throwing rocks into your harbours because someone else had done the same to theirs. But the proposition that a tariff could enrich a country by improving its terms of trade, first suggested by John Stuart Mill in 1829, proved impregnable to assault. Mill's argument rested on the unproblematic assumption that the international market was imperfectly competitive. If so anything, including a tariff, which restricted your demand for imports would cut their price relative to that of your exports.[2] In strict economic terms, the theory did not even rule out putting on tariffs against free traders. Bilateral free trade was always better than bilateral protection, but that was the limit of the theory's assistance to commercial policy.

Mill realised that any gain from the improved terms of trade might be outweighed by a welfare loss through the reduced volume of trade. For this reason, among others, he was notably reluctant to support a policy of reciprocity, negotiation or retaliation over tariffs.[3]

Robert Torrens, who arrived at a similar theory independently of Mill, was less cautious. To the 'supply-side' argument he added the proposition that any country which took off tariffs unilaterally would incur a trade deficit which would reduce the stock of money. This would not only threaten a slump but reduce the price of all the country's goods, including exports. The terms of trade would deteriorate a second time.

But Torrens (despite a decisive and very public victory over Nassau Senior in 1843–4) counted for little as first the Whigs, then the Peelite faction of the Tories, and finally the Tory protectionist rump under Lord Derby announced their conversion to free trade. No theoretical case for reciprocity could alter the fact that the policy had so clearly failed in practice. Surveying the tangle of treaties and most-favoured nation agreements since the end of the Napoleonic Wars, Whigs and Tories alike concluded that Britain had got very little indeed for her pains. The Whig government which succeeded Peel after his repeal of the Corn Laws set about the systematic removal of imperial preference from Britain's commercial policy, as well as repealing the Navigation Laws. A minority Conservative government in 1852 revived the principle of reciprocity when it came near to securing a bilateral treaty with France, but was out of office within months, to make way for Gladstone's great free-trading budget of 1853. The principle that tariffs were just another form of indirect tax, and must compete with the others to justify their existence, had been an article of Whig doctrine for ten years or more. Now it was a Peelite Chancellor enshrining it at the centre of his budget.

Palmerston's first ministry (1855–8) negotiated some minor treaties outside Europe, but when he returned to office in 1859 with Gladstone, now a Liberal, as his Chancellor, the push towards freer trade was determined and immediate. Its first result was Cobden's commercial treaty of 1860 with France. To the many purists still alive in the Liberal Party, any such treaty was more a betrayal than an extension of free trade. Palmerston himself admitted that it was 'not easy for us to explain why we revert to the exploded system of a treaty about tariffs without saying it was the choice of the French government'.[4]

But Gladstone's attitude, in private as well as in public, was far more robust. In a letter to his friend, Sir James Lacaita, he commended the treaty not 'for mere increase of trade [but] for those blessings which increase of trade brings with it: peace, security, goodwill';[5] while in parliament he made the rather fine distinction between a reciprocal arrangement, which the treaty was, and a bargain, which it was not. A bargain involved each side giving something away which they would otherwise have chosen to retain: in the treaty, by contrast, 'you are giving nothing to France that is not a gift to yourself, and you are receiving nothing from France except measures by which France confers a benefit on herself'.[6] In his budget speech on 10 February 1860 Gladstone easily avoided the question of whether he would have brought in the same budget without a French treaty. Apart from anything else, no one asked him. However, at one point he did seem to be saying that he would have done it all the same way except for cutting the duty on brandy.[7]

Gladstone's speech won many critics round.[8] Lowe himself, as we shall see, was distinctly softened by it. And some unilateralists were placated by the way Britain made its reductions in tariffs applicable to all countries, not to mention the most-favoured-nation clause ensuring that Britain would benefit from any subsequent treaties signed by France with third parties. The treaty was intended as, and would succeed in becoming, the basis of a network of agreements across Europe, led and orchestrated by Britain and France, and interlocked through further most-favoured-nation clauses. Nonetheless, the consensus in February 1860 was that its rationale was more political and diplomatic than economic. Clarendon said as much in his admission that 'The treaty is thoroughly unsound, and a great mistake [but] rejecting it, making an enemy of the Emperor... would be a far greater mistake.'[9] A retrospective Gladstone was to be blunter still: 'There were only two alternatives, one of them the French treaty and the other war with France.'[10]

II

Even if he had not been outside the cabinet, the vice-president of the Board of Education would have been one of the lesser weights as Palmerston's government oversaw the treaty with France. But the vice-president was leading a double life, odd even by the more relaxed standards of the time, as chief critic of the treaty in the leader columns of *The Times*. Even odder, and highly uncharacteristic of Lowe, was the chief critic's habit of reversing his position almost weekly.

These editorials can be taken as an accurate and unconstrained version of Lowe's shifting personal opinions. John Thaddeus Delane, Lowe's friend and ex-pupil at Oxford who edited the paper throughout Lowe's period as a leader-writer, thought Lowe was well able to 'shoot his own arrows' behind the shield of *The Times*, and his correspondence with Lowe confirms this.[11] Lowe's oscillation was between four different positions. The treaty, consistently, was founded on faulty political economy, but

1. this condemned it *per se*
2. it was to be condemned even if it had not been founded on faulty political economy
3. it should however be approved for non-economic reasons
4. it was still an economic improvement on no treaty.

Lowe started in the third position. *The Times*, he wrote on 16 January 1860, was

> not disposed, as at present advised, to regard with favour any proposition for a return to the exploded practice of negotiating commercial treaties, but as to the general character of the measure sketched out, there can be no difference of opinion, at least on this side of the Channel.

In other words he was for it. Why, if the practice had been rightly exploded? Because, said Lowe, peace came before even political economy, and anything which freed up trade promoted peace. Bring Anglo-French trade up to the levels of Anglo-US trade, and you will have rendered war 'absolutely impossible'.[12]

A week later Lowe pulled himself together with a biting diatribe against the treaty. Among those bitten was Robert Lowe no. 3. Now Lowe no. 1 related how he had supposed that England, no longer being a child, had put away childish things. Instead the government was making war on political economy, which rightly ruled that tariffs were justified only to collect revenue. To negotiate with France over tariffs made no more sense than negotiating with France over what your poor rate should be.

It was in this editorial that Lowe made his sole fleeting reference to Torrens' case for reciprocity, based on the demonstration that unilateral removal of tariffs could make a country poorer by worsening its terms of trade. Lowe merely commented that reciprocity was 'the last colour that is assumed by the dying dolphin of Protection', and that, though Torrens' arguments for it were 'not entirely without force', they were overwhelmed by the case for deciding 'our own taxation in strict accordance with abstract science'. Moreover, commercial treaties actually obstructed free trade: 'If we are to have commercial treaties we shall negotiate at the greatest possible disadvantage unless we have imposed on ourselves most exorbitant duties.' Finally, after observing that a trade treaty with protectionist France was like a treaty of religious toleration with the Pope, Lowe took up the argument that, if the treaty gave our coal and iron access to France, only a pedant would complain about its misalignment with economic correctness. But who were the real economic obsessives here, Lowe asked. The opponents of the treaty, or supporters who could think only of export earnings as they furnished a belligerent France with 'the two most important elements of war – coal and iron'?[13]

The treaty now emerged in a very odd fashion. Gladstone's budget of February 1860 spelt out nearly everything that Britain was 'conceding', as Lowe would not have put it. In a few cases, including coal, France too specified its new tariff. But in general all that the French were promising was that prohibitions of British imports would be replaced by duties not exceeding 30 per cent. The actual level of these duties would be announced unilaterally by France once she had investigated, industry by industry, what was needed to 'equalise the conditions under which domestic and foreign producers worked'.[14] Britain, with its own 'offer' set out, had no threats or promises left to try and influence this process. Its manufacturers might be invited over to Paris to assist the French investigation, but in the end all Britain could do was check the French facts and figures and doubt their accuracy when convenient (which Cobden duly did in the autumn of 1860).[15]

In fact all this was a carefully planned sequence which suited both sides well. The French emperor was anxious to sign the treaty before its opponents, whose formidable powers of agitation he had already experienced, had time to organise themselves;[16] while the British government were whittling down the apparent element of reciprocity and thus blunting the weapons of their unilateralist critics.

Certainly Lowe was not in a very strong position to condemn the order of play which, after all, largely divorced the detailed proposals of each side from his demons of negotiation, promise and threat. On the other hand, he may have felt that a treaty which legitimised these evils just by being a treaty, only to hand to France all the strategic advantages of declaring last, got the worst of all possible worlds. Such ambiguities in his mind would help to explain why his tergiverisations now picked up speed. Initially, in the wake of Gladstone's budget, Lowe softened once again, even (27 February 1860) crediting the treaty with improving British perceptions of France to the point where 'instead of regarding her as a storehouse of every possible danger and mischief, we are now beginning to look upon her as a magazine of many good things, as a land whose wine we shall drink, whose manufactures we shall improve'. He then changed his position a third time, back to unqualified hostility. By May he was condemning exactly the unilateralist aspects of the treaty which might have helped him reconcile to it. Britain, he said, was unambiguously cutting duties against France, and whether she got anything in return would 'depend solely on the favour and generosity of our magnanimous ally'.[17] And by August he was saying he had known all along that 'we were bound to get the worst' from the 'huckstering negotiation' which had so successfully returned Britain to the days when politics had been mixed up with finance.

Political economy was now re-enthroned as the sole arbiter of trading policy. It forbade negotiating over tariffs and that was that. 'The truths of science are no more fitting subjects for international compact than the dictates of morality.' But instead of following political economy, we had followed 'the wisdom of Mr Gladstone, which is wisdom of another fashion from that of Adam Smith, Ricardo and Mill'. Not the least damage done by Gladstone's wisdom was the revival of the business attitude which blamed the government for all its troubles. Commercial circulars which blamed the treaty for slackness of trade might well be right. The point, however, was that blaming the government invariably preceded an extension of its role – quite apart from the 'degradation' of merchants who had gone to Paris to beg favours from a foreign power. Whether the 'peace' argument might still have trumped Adam Smith for Lowe is unclear because he now abandoned it. If this is a treaty for peace, he asked, why had we just raised defence spending by another £1.2 million to protect ourselves from France?[18]

At the end of 1860 the final details of the French side of the treaty were published. Gladstone must have been gratified by Lowe's response that it might all have been a lot worse: 'we have paid dear for this treaty but we cannot deny that we have got something to show for our money'. But not as much as France, whose gains were beyond narrow financial calculation. Prohibitionist France had been a brave and confident nation hobbled by an unfounded and uncharacteristic timidity about the quality of her goods. But now, Lowe believed, all this would give way. 'Limited competition will give confidence, and confidence will in its turn whet the appetite for more competition.'[19]

How right he had been about this, claimed Lowe, when in 1862 he reviewed the treaty's first two years. The grief of the French protectionists, far more avid to be proved right than to see their country prosper, only added to the satisfaction everyone else ought to be feeling.

> We can no longer recognise in the French Protectionist the light-hearted inhabitant of the beautiful land of the orange and vine – the gay, gallant, thoughtless cavalier, ever ready to set Europe in a blaze, and to dance gaily round the conflagration. There is a deep and guttural emphasis in the growl with which the French Protectionist receives every fresh development of Free Trade, which assures us that there must be some very solid prosperity at the bottom of so much ostentatious discomfort.[20]

After this final flourish Lowe no. 4 took charge and was never again dislodged. His final editorial on the subject provided his strongest statement that once the truths of political economy were understood, all sides would rush to remove duties unilaterally and 'we shall hear no more of Treaties of Commerce'.[21]

Even with a writer as invigorating as Lowe, it would be tedious to chronicle every remark he made about the Cobden treaty, and we have not done so. We have, however, charted the twisting road he followed on an ordnance survey rather than a motoring map, because its details possess a significance larger than Lowe's own career. It is as much a fact today as in 1860 that, in matters of commercial policy, it is the dogmatic free traders who are the least robust while the more malleable folk, paradoxically, take a course of stern resolve. And this is because commercial treaties, just by being treaties, pose a nigh-insuperable dilemma for Ricardian economics. One horn we have seen – you cannot negotiate without encouraging the delusion that unilateral tariff-cutting is a sacrifice, rather than an economic gain regardless of what anyone else does. The other horn, however, is that cutting tariffs unilaterally *is* a sacrifice if, in doing so, you give up the chance to persuade others, however misguided their logic, to follow suit. In the end, therefore, it is the convinced free traders who take out the weights and the balance every time some detail within the situation changes, while those less certain, or less comprehending, of the Ricardian message forge blithely ahead with agreements on wine and multifibres, wheat and microprocessors. Anyone cognisant with, say, the modern *Economist* magazine's attitude to the World Trade Organisation, will feel on familiar ground as they read about the 1860 treaty and Lowe.

Lowe was on much firmer ground (indeed his voice would be a salutary one today) in his enthusiastic demolition of the neo-mercantilist idea that trade surpluses were good and deficits bad. An import he recommended to all nations was the ideas of Adam Smith, which would both stop *Le Moniteur* exulting over France's trade surplus with England[22] and, more important, instil some sense into the USA's protectionist North for as long as the Civil War deprived it of the free-trading wisdom of the Confederacy.[23] France's surplus was a matter for commiseration: 'We want to turn the balance of trade against us because we want to buy cheap and sell dear.'[24] And when disgruntled French protectionists claimed the treaty was increasing their imports of British machinery, Lowe told them to celebrate, not complain. Obviously, the British machines were better than their own, or they would not be importing them.[25] It was not a surprise, however, if many French were taking mercantilist attitudes, in the light of a treaty which, simply by *being* a commercial treaty, 'gave the high authority of England to the popular fallacy that it is better to export than to import'.[26] If you spent 14 years making unilateral cuts in duty, with the (correct) implication that import was more desirable than export, and then signed an agreement implying the exact opposite, what foreigner would not become confused?

Later in 1863 the confusion seemed to be spreading to Britain's two most august free traders. Cobden and Bright had now gone beyond merely urging the government to help Indian producers bring on a larger supply of cotton, which was being done, and with Lowe's approval, given the emergency of the American cotton famine.[27] Now they were insisting that the Secretary for India put pressure on the ryots 'with a view to induce or compel them to grow a larger amount of cotton than they are at present disposed to produce'. Cobden, indeed, had admitted that on this occasion he was throwing free trade to the winds. And why? Because the ryot was ignorant of his own best interests:

> ignorant, we must suppose to an extent which prevents him knowing what crop will pay him best. Even if this is so – which it is not – that is no reason for depriving him of the disposition of his labour and capital, and reducing him virtually to the condition of a slave.[28]

III

Lowe's enthusiasm for the Board of Trade did not long survive his own departure from it in 1858. Where he had praised it as the graveyard of reciprocity, he now accused it of planning a mass exhumation. The trigger was a parliamentary committee's recommendation that, in matters of commercial diplomacy, 'the Board of Trade be placed more nearly upon an equality with the Foreign Office than it is at present'. This, to Lowe, was a retrograde move to placate a retrograde institution. The Board had been established

> at a time when it was a received axiom of political science that it was the duty of the government to regulate, promote and protect the trade of its own country. But I really thought we had got to the end of these things . . . that the time had come . . . when the entire business which the Government might have with the trade of the country be described by the pithy axiom of Lord Melbourne 'Why can't you leave it alone?'[29]

Rather than raise the status of the Board, Lowe proposed abolishing its 'consultative department', that is the part which assisted the Foreign Office with commercial treaties. Lowe used the occasion to repeat his standard criticisms of commercial treaties, plus a new one – that so few tariffs were left that an agreement which depended on 'giving things away' was impractical as well as improper. 'It is as if a person should go into a shop to purchase goods for ready money but should first throw his purse into the Thames.'[30]

At the end of 1865 all these arguments gained a new focus – the proposed commercial treaty with Austria. But in the meantime, Lowe had used parliament and *The Times* to mount radical challenges in two disparate areas – intellectual property and the economics of the cattle plague (Rinderpest) of 1865.

Lowe's first critique of patent law in fact dated from 1861, when he left it to the government to look at it and decide if it should be abolished. But he left no doubt that he thought the laws did more harm than good. Not only were a large number of inventions patented but never developed, stopping someone else developing them; in addition, people who did not *want* the expense and trouble of patenting their inventions had to do so, for fear that someone else would exclude them. It would be different if the law were really needed to reward the long process of discovery and development but, said Lowe, most of the ideas patented had not involved years of thought and expense. Patents were not needed to bring them about.[31]

Lowe came back to the subject in 1864, adding another layer of arguments against regulation. Patent monopolies seldom rewarded the most deserving inventions or even went to the actual inventor. Instead 'the law mulcts the whole community to reward one person, and large fortunes are gained by alterations made in the shape of a hairbrush or the sole of a clog'. This might happen either before or after the 'endless litigation before a judge and jury unqualified to understand the case', while, in the rare cases where the inventor collected his own reward, it was frequently at future inventors' expense. All too often, the perfection of an invention required the use of other inventions already patented by someone else.[32]

As for the Rinderpest, Lowe and John Stuart Mill found themselves jousting over the as-yet-unenunciated concept of elasticity of demand. The clash arose from the narrower but more urgent issue of who, if anyone, should compensate the farmers whose animals had been destroyed in order to try and contain the plague. Mill wanted a brand new 'poll tax on cattle', so that the whole farming community, and only the farming community, might bear the burden of relieving their unlucky brothers. Acton Smee Ayrton MP said this was taxing the victims to compensate the victims. No, retorted Mill: the disaster had already raised the price of meat and milk, so that the general public were losing and the unaffected farmers actually gaining. To compensate the affected farmers through general taxation would thus be unjust to the general taxpayer.[33]

Mr Mill, replied Lowe, 'is, I am afraid, a little too clever for us in this House'.

> Where does the hon. Gentleman find, in any work of political economy that in a case like the present, where great losses are incurred by a class, which losses diminish the supply of a certain article, that necessarily the class will be indemnified by increased prices?[34]

Apart from anything else, much of the gain would go to foreign suppliers. This forced Mill to be more exact. Lowe was quite right, he said, to point out that 'the scarcity of the commodity does not always raise the price in full proportion to the deficiency of the commodity'. But it might raise the price by more, and in the case of a necessity like milk, would certainly do so.[35] However striking the spectacle of Lowe of all people leading a pitchfork resistance to the intelligentsia, the cold eye of a modern economist cannot agree with the contemporary verdict of a Lowe win on points. All the same, no other member during Mill's three years in parliament even sought to correct him on political economy, let alone corner him into replacing a condescending inexactitude with a glimmer of neoclassical rigour.

Thus satisfied, Lowe turned back to damning the Austrian treaty. Its reciprocal nature worked him up into a retrospective condemnation of its French counterpart, which he had apparently finally settled down to tolerating, but which was now part of the process in which Britain had 'dragged down this great subject from the dignity of a science to the foggy regions of diplomacy', while 'weary[ing] all Europe with our entreaties to enter into commercial agreements'.[36] Moreover, Lowe changed his mind yet again about whether such agreements would promote or prevent peace. Swinging back to pessimism, he opined that more treaties meant more breaches of treaty, with every breach a *casus belli*. Nor did treaties need to be breached to be dangerous. Inevitably they raised hopes of political and diplomatic concord which could not be satisfied, leaving the two 'partners' more antagonistic than before. This was especially likely with Austria. Serious cuts in the duties Austria paid would leave Britain with too little revenue to fund government spending. But the less Austria could expect economically from the treaty, the more she would expect politically, and the harder the feelings when she failed to get it.[37]

British criticism of the French treaty, as often from a protectionist standpoint as from Lowe's, rumbled on through the 1860s, and in 1870 Lowe, now Chancellor, was faced with a demand that it be referred to a parliamentary committee. The treaty was due to expire after ten years or when either side denounced it, whichever was the later; now Hugh Birley, Conservative MP for Manchester, was claiming that exports to France had performed so poorly under the treaty that parliament ought to investigate why, with a view to renegotiation on more favourable terms.

Exports to France had in fact almost doubled, though it was true that France retained a substantial trade surplus with Britain. But, in any case, to replace one treaty with another, with the British position driven by mercantilist pleading, was an option hardly likely to appeal to Lowe. He replied that first, protection did not work even in protectionist terms, sheltered industries typically becoming so inefficient that exports suffered more than imports; and secondly (a favourite point) that even granting such a committee would help fix in businessmen's heads the idea that government could cure the reverses of trade. Expectations would thus be raised that could never be fulfilled; the government would then incur odium that was quite undeserved; in short 'no more fatal delusion can be considered'.[38]

Lowe was at the same time privately renewing his demand that the Board of Trade should lose its responsibilities for commercial treaties to the Foreign Office. (A parliamentary inquiry eventually sided with him, Gladstone agreed and it was done.) The trigger was John Bright, who in cabinet had sprung upon an unprepared Lowe the proposal to set up a joint committee of Board of Trade and Treasury officials to inquire if a cut in the duty on wine would facilitate treaties with Spain and Portugal. To Lowe this was simply one department of government 'getting up agitation' against another. As Chancellor *he* decided what the duty on wine should be, and did not expect then to have to 'refer my own decision to two persons in my department and one in the Board of Trade... unless I am to have the support of *every* department of the Government in maintaining Taxation I do not see how I can acquit myself of my arduous responsibilities'.[39]

At least things had improved for Lowe in one respect. In the early 1860s he had attacked commercial treaties for sustaining tariffs above their legitimate, revenue-raising level. (He thought they did this, as we have seen, because governments wanted to have as much as possible to 'give away' during negotiations.) Now he feared that a treaty with Spain would push tariffs too low for the Treasury to cope. The days were gone when tariff reductions might increase total revenue. The worst tariffs were long dead, with the result that the economy was no longer on the sunny side of the Laffer curve. It was gratifying in a way that taxes had fallen to the point where inadequate revenue could be the main fear.[40]

Lowe was being disingenuous so far as some of his own tax cuts, as Chancellor, might have been used to secure reciprocal concessions. Germany and Belgium had both signified willingness to cut tariffs if Britain would lower her duties on tobacco and sugar. Lowe did both – but unilaterally and without consultation – in his first two budgets. This was seen, correctly, as a sign that Lowe's unilateralism was winning the argument within Gladstone's government.[41] Ill health removed Bright from the Board of Trade in December 1870. Gladstone himself weighed into the debate on the future of the French treaty with a long memorandum to the effect that all the anti-treaty arguments of 1860, and none of the pro-treaty ones, were still out in full strength.[42]

Lowe worked hard to hold Gladstone to this position, recounting how in the cabinet which saw Bright's ambush (Gladstone was absent) he had 'quoted you as to the real nature of the French treaty'.[43] But his fears remained that Liberal as well as Conservative politicians would press for a revision of the French treaty and that the Board of Trade would connive with them. In the event it was the French who took the initiative. Thiers, who came to power after the fall of the Commune in 1871, was a veteran protectionist who had recently supported a campaign to have the Emperor denounce the treaty. Moreover he badly needed new revenues to pay for the cost of the war and the indemnity to Germany. (Surprisingly this argument cut more ice in Britain than in France.) In August 1871 Thiers told Britain to choose between a modified treaty more favourable to France or no treaty at all. But, unlike Louis Napoleon ten years earlier, Thiers quickly found himself to be more protectionist than much

French commercial opinion, which had largely come round to support of the 1860 treaty. In the end France and Britain agreed on a replacement treaty which raised a limited number of duties above their 1860 level. This fell with Thiers in May 1873, and the new agreement which followed effectively restored the 1860 treaty with few changes. Gladstone backed the treaty, like its predecessor, on largely diplomatic grounds, making it clear in private that his misgivings about the reciprocity principle had been hardened by the conduct of the French.[44] So had Lowe's, if such a thing were possible; and, unlike Gladstone, he showed no inclination to view the new treaty from a diplomatic angle, rather complaining that the Foreign Office had shut him as Chancellor out of the negotiations.[45]

Lowe's last and most sustained look at free trade appeared in *Nineteenth Century* in June 1878. 'Reciprocity and Free Trade' was a sharp attack on self-styled free traders who were nothing of the kind. A Mr Wallace, to whom Lowe was responding, had said that free trade should be limited if the resulting mines and furnaces threatened a country's natural beauty. Lowe simply exiled such aesthetic considerations from political economy. They had no more to do with it than 'whether a man likes to spend his money in growing tulips or in feeding pigs'.[46] Wallace had further suggested that tit-for-tat retaliation, whereby you placed the same duties on the same industries as you faced yourself was not only desirable, but closer to free trade than unilateral tariff-cutting. Lowe retorted that this policy was ineffective even in Wallace's own terms. Tariffs were imposed by a country which could not compete in that particular industry on the country that could: what was the point of using the same industry to retaliate? Instead, Lowe concluded sarcastically, we should retaliate

> not upon what our adversary cannot, but what he can, sell to a profit in our country, and thus introducing into our intercourse with civilised and on the whole friendly nations, the principle on which war is founded – the bringing of enormous evils on ourselves in the hope of inflicting still greater evils on our rivals.[47]

IV

Free Trade to Lowe was the issue *par excellence* to drive home the scientific status of political economy. And 'scientific' meant mathematical and irrefutable, not empirical and falsifiable. Thus doubters over the efficacy of abolishing the Corn Laws were people who

> applied principles drawn from political experience to economical science. They forget that they had passed out of that region of compromise and conjecture in which the politician is ever doomed to dwell, and got into the region of absolute truth, which works out the conditions deducible from its premises with something very nearly approaching to mathematical precision.[48]

The abolitionists in contrast had realised exactly what political economy was, had applied it to the issue in hand, and so had rightly 'dealt more in abstract and general principles than any speeches that ever were addressed to a large multitude'.[49] Naturally, this could be only as effective as the mental limits of the multitude allowed. And inevitably, some protectionists would congratulate the backward section of the working class, elevating their stupidity into a hard-headed refusal to be seduced by abstractions. Lowe feared that scientific truth would remain the preserve of the 'classes qualified by education to comprehend'. True, those who could not manage the principles might be converted by experiencing the benefits of free trade. 'Nature makes Protectionists, knowledge and observation freetraders.' But this was a slow business, with an implacable protectionist enemy: 'death, which mows down day by day the ripened harvest of education and experience'.[50]

In his editorials discussing the nature and appeal of free trade, Lowe foreshadowed a number of themes which were to dominate his political and intellectual career: absolutism in economics; empiricism as a useful second string for convincing those unable to accept the *a priori* certainties which were the real political economy; pessimism about popular understanding of economic issues. In fact, said Lowe, the working class was so bound to be wrong that it was better for it not to try to understand political economy at all:

> Democracy cannot govern. There are some questions on which democracy will hear no reason. It happily is not always able to rise to the consideration of anything so abstract as the principles of political economy; but when it attempts it, is invariably wrong. We owe the repeal of the Corn Laws, not to the appreciation by

> the working-classes of the superiority of the claims of the consumer to those of the producer, but to the incredible folly of the advocates of protection in linking their cause with the odious imposition of a bread tax.[51]

Mixing up political economy with politics, then, was a fate Lowe warmly wished on his enemies. It was his allies – or those who should have been – whom he chastised for the sin. Gladstone was a target more than once,[52] but was spared the full rigour of the treatment handed out to Bright in 1860.

Bright had told the Wakefield Mechanics Institution's annual soiree that political economy 'has been practised for 100 years and is still absolutely in its infancy'. It was the art of turning political economy into sound policy that was in its infancy, retorted Lowe, and Bright's own ignorance of the fundamental principles of legislation fitted him perfectly to demonstrate the point, albeit not in the way he thought he was doing. Anyone who thought that money handed over in tax 'is as much lost to the people as if it were thrown into the sea' (Lowe was ever-assiduous in quoting opponents out of context) should ask London dockers if their pay-packets might be consigned to the Thames without repercussion. As for the government's 'duty' to lift the poor out of poverty, if only Bright had consulted the infant science, he would have learned that government cannot have the duty, because it does not have the power, to raise anyone from poverty to wealth. In fact, said Lowe, a theory which had so far outstripped its proper application to human affairs (witness, once again, poor Bright) must be, not in its infancy, but in 'a very forward state of development'.[53] Lowe did not try to elucidate the circumstances in which ignorant humanity would or would not hit on eternal economic truths and translate them into law; what rather tied his analysis together was his complete confidence that once good economic laws were enacted, however accidentally, ex post facto perception of their overwhelming merits would make them unassailable.

> [This] kind of law, of which history unhappily affords us very few examples, is founded on abstract truth, which it brings for the first time prominently and practically before the world. Its influence strengthens with its duration, clamour and prejudice are hushed and die out, and that which was at first mistaken for a more local

> and temporary arrangement is recognised in its true character as a rule of universal utility, a solid step onward in the progress of the human race.
>
> Such a law – we may now say without contradiction – was the Bank Charter Act of 1844.[54]

In this passage at least, Lowe is firmly on J.S. Mill's agenda, namely that the economist's task is to discover the conditions of application of economic doctrines. (Prediction as the purpose of economics was to come much later, and get Lowe into much posthumous trouble.) Unlike Mill, however, Lowe thought it transparent that economists and the economy had been working together steadily to broaden these conditions of application. Thus when in 1864 he accused even Adam Smith of faint-heartedness, he also implied that Smith's date of birth was both explanation and excuse:

> Nothing proves more clearly the title of political economy to the dignity of a science than the fact that the better it is understood and the more its abstract deductions are tested by experience, the more general and the better they become. The theory came from its great author hampered with many exceptions, but the course of inquiry, which so often leads to the introduction of exceptions to general rules, has tended in this instance to prove that they never ought to have been made. That the doctrines of Free trade do not apply to agriculture, that the interest of money ought not, like every other price, to be permitted to regulate itself according to demand and supply and, above all, that shipping should be secured to a country by the exclusion of foreign competition, are all heresies which have been held by distinguished men and sanctioned by great names, but which have been successively demolished by the power of reason and opinion, leaving the place they once took up to be occupied by the wide principles the application of which they have vainly sought to circumscribe.[55]

But just as it took time to see the true merits of laws which enshrined the principles of political economy, so an economy could survive for a while with laws that transgressed them, as Lowe pointed out in 1862 when, in the American Civil War, the Union made the dollar inconvertible and yet their financial system did not immediately collapse. Lowe's comment is so good a summary of his lifelong attitude to political economy that it is worth quoting at length.

> It is easy for a person moderately versed in the laws of economical science to apply abstract principles to undoubted facts, and to draw from them conclusions in which he feels the most perfect confidence. But the realisation of these conclusions as a fact must depend on numberless circumstances of which general and abstract speculation can take no account. The laws of political economy are sure ultimately to assert themselves, but the laws of political economy are, after all, only the laws of the human mind, and the predictions of the future which the science enables us to make are founded on the supposition that those laws take their uniform and usual course. Political economy assumes that mankind, taken in the mass and in the long run, will act according to that which they believe to be their true interest; but political economy makes no allowance for all those things which blind men as to what their true interest is – vanity, patriotism, loyalty, hope, ambition, imagination, with all their exaggerating and distorting powers, are banished from the creed of the dismal science. These things tend to modify conclusions and to retard the action of general principles, but how far they do this every speculator must investigate and consider for himself.[56]

In 1862 John Stuart Mill was as much the standard point of reference for the philosophy of economics as for economics itself. In *A System of Logic* (1843) he had argued that the principles of economics are subject to appropriate conditions of application, but held out no certainty that these will eventually come about in any given context. The passage quoted above does possess such certainty: Lowe believes the action of general principles can at most be 'retarded'. And there are two further departures from Mill's methodological position. First, while Lowe's political economy 'makes no allowance' for non-economic motives, Mill believed it *must* make such allowance if it were to influence the public and guide the legislator. It might be argued that the difference is definitional: the responsibilities Mill lays on political economy are laid by Lowe on the individual 'speculator'. The end product is the same: what does it matter what is nominally placed within the definition of political economy and what the user is told he is required to add to it? But the second and greater difference between Lowe and Mill cannot be dissolved into semantics. The non-economic motives which both believe to be so important are, nonetheless, to Lowe, illusions which 'blind men as to what their true interest is'. It is one thing to say that patriotism or loyalty induce altruistic actions which may disrupt economic theories. It is quite another to take a lumpenmarxist line that these feelings are a form of 'false consciousness'. What Lowe probably meant was not that a patriot was a deluded fool – his own patriotic sentiments were often on display – but that patriotic sentiments, like everything else, do not endure in the same way as do the imperatives of economic interest.

After Lowe's prolonged and strident celebrations of the deductive method in political economy, his use of the Reform proposals of 1865–7 to damn *a priori* methods in politics itself may have caused surprise. It would not have done so, however, to anyone familiar with the article on 'The Past Session and the New Parliament' which Lowe had written in 1857. Much of this piece is a prolonged crow of delight at the voters' recent massacre of the Manchester dogmatists in parliament. Large numbers of Liberal MPs elected in 1852, said Lowe, had 'traded on the single profession of the doctrines of Free Trade'.[57] Their influence had been 'mischievous and impractical', and the main reason why parliament's authority had declined.[58] But now Manchester itself was free of the 'intolerable oppression' of the Manchester school.

> A heavy blow has been struck at that crotchety, useless class of politicians, who, being perplexed with uneasy consciences, insist on viewing every question on its abstract merits...Men who refuse to look at practical questions from [a] practical point of view have mistaken their vocation when they enter public life.[59]

This was consistent with the view Lowe was to take in the Reform debates of the 1860s. His preface to his *Speeches and Letters on Reform* contrasted the 'mostly metaphysical' arguments for democracy with his own side's arguments, 'all drawn, or profess[ing] to be drawn from considerations purely practical'.[60] And:

> When I find a book or a speech appealing to abstract a priori principles I put it aside in despair, being well aware that I can

> learn nothing useful from it. Such works only present to us the limited and qualified propositions which experience has established, without their limits and qualifications, and elevate them into principles by a rash generalisation which strips them of whatever truth they originally possessed.[61]

But why was Lowe excoriating in the realm of politics exactly the kind of methods he had just been celebrating so loudly in economics? His answer was that he was a pragmatist, choosing for each discipline the method that worked best. But what determined what worked best? And what exactly does 'worked best' mean anyway? Lowe was to answer both questions in his methodological clash with the English historical school, as recounted in Chapter 12.

4
Education, Education, Administration

It was 'a great Economical Truth', said Lowe, that 'Education is no exception to the rules of Political Economy.'[1] What he meant was that education should be subject to the principles of Adam Smith. And, like Smith, he contrasted free economical Scotland with politicised, endowment-ridden England. 'In Scotland', said Lowe, 'they sell education like a grocer sells figs'.[2]

This was praise. And, because it was praise, and because of Lowe's attempts to introduce payment by results to England as well, he acquired an odium among educationists that lasted well into the twentieth century. A number of dissertations in teacher training colleges in the 1950s and 1960s homed in on Lowe as an archetypal Gradgrind, bent on cutting out anything which might feed the childish imagination, so that costs might be cut and returns precisely quantified. D.W. Sylvester's *Robert Lowe on Education* (1974) was a long-overdue corrective to this wilfully blinkered – and deservedly unpublished – view of Lowe.

But before coming on to what Lowe thought children should learn, how far the state should influence what they learned and how it might go about it, let us place him, as he deserves and would have wished, firmly in the Smithian tradition. Smith, famously, had said that competition in education was necessary given the teacher's desire, shared with the rest of mankind, to live as much at ease as he could. Educational endowments were an evil since they gratified this desire. J.S. Mill agreed, and so did Lowe.

> Those ... who seek to work out education on the basis of endowments deliberately reject a superior machine in order to avail themselves of an inferior one. There is no occupation more likely to degenerate into lifeless routine and meaningless repetition.[3]

If this were the standard to which endowed schools sank, one might expect the competition of unencumbered schools to drive them out of business, in which case the problem would solve itself. No, said Lowe: quite apart from the incontestable fact that this had not happened, he would never have expected it to happen. The endowed schools did not just undersell their competitors, but deterred entry in the first place.

> What they actually do, we see, and for that they get full credit. What they prevent others from doing we do not see, and consequently do not reflect upon: but the agency of endowment is just as real in preventing better teaching as in teaching badly itself.[4]

Endowment by the government was as bad as any other form: a principle Lowe was to find useful as Chancellor of the Exchequer. When the Meteorological Society of Scotland applied to him for help, they were probably unsurprised at his refusal. The lecture on education may have been more unexpected. The moment people who found schools 'begin to finger government money', Lowe told them, their scholarly intentions die, vanquished by the urge to milk the government for even more. The implication – though even Lowe stopped short of saying it blatantly – was that the Scottish meteorological society would do exactly the same.[5]

II

On becoming vice-president of the Board of education in 1859, Lowe did not take over a public system of education as the twenty-first century would understand it; indeed he did not 'take over' the education system at all. Not for another 11 years would the State even ensure that every child had access to a school. Its role was to supervise, inspect and, to a very limited extent, subsidise schools.

Education subsidised but not free of charge was a principle all classical economists had supported, from Adam Smith to John Stuart

Mill. But in his final pronouncement on education, in 1869, Mill *would* call for free secondary education for those capable of benefiting from it. And, even by 1859, Mill was demanding that education be compulsory while sounding a crescendo of dissatisfaction both with the standards in voluntary schools and with the ability of parents to choose the right one for their children.[6]

Lowe however, like Smith, thought parents, not teachers or civil servants, were the best judges of a good school. Naturally they would make mistakes but 'their faults are mainly the corrigible faults of ignorance, not of apathy and prejudice'.[7] And the fees would help them conquer their ignorance; Lowe even suggested that the expense would lead not just to better schooling but more schooling, as the price conferred a subjective value on the commodity. 'There is no greater security for getting parents to send their children to school than requiring them to pay for it.'[8] Lowe again remained true to Adam Smith when the Schools Inquiry Commission of 1868 asked his view on the idea of licensing schoolteachers. 'I suppose', asked the chairman, 'you would not consider that the educational profession should be put on the same grounds as the medical profession?' Lowe replied that, far from licensing teachers, there was a case for unlicensing doctors: 'I myself doubt exceedingly the policy of the medical Act. There are plenty of quacks inside.'[9]

As vice-president of the Board of Education at the Privy Council between 1859 and 1864 – the 'vice' is honorary, Lowe was the equivalent of a modern Secretary of State – Lowe had the chance to put his ideas into practice. During his tenure he never wavered in his intention to apply political economy to education. And the main result of this was the Revised Code of 1862.

Under the Revised Code teachers' pay was brought under the laws of supply and demand. The Board of Education stepped aside and teachers concluded local, even individual, bargains with their school managers. But far more radical than even this step was Lowe's scheme for paying schools by their results. Each school was to receive two grants per pupil. The first was for attendance: four shillings for the year if the child had attended 200 morning or afternoon sessions, otherwise nothing. The second was an eight-shilling grant conditional on the child passing examinations in arithmetic, reading and writing, 2s. 8d. to be deducted for each subject failed.

The idea was not wholly new. The Department of Science and Art (now also Lowe's responsibility) had been paying schools by results, where art and science instruction was involved, since 1856. What was new was Lowe's determination that kindly inspectors, loath to enforce payment by results, should no longer obstruct the principle. Under the new code inspectors would be forced to abide by the examination requirements.

Critics – then and later – claimed Lowe's real objective was to reduce government spending on education. Lowe never expected this, and refused to predict whether the Revised Code would even slow down the rate of increase. Instead he promised the Commons that it would be either cheap or efficient. 'The present is neither one nor the other. If the schools do not give instruction the public money will not be demanded, but if instruction is given the public money will be demanded – I cannot say what amount, but the public will get value for money.'[10]

Lowe also vigorously denied the charge that, because he had chosen the three Rs for examination, he must think nothing else mattered. The subjects to be examined, he told his Permanent Secretary, represented 'an amount of knowledge which could be ascertained thoroughly by examination. Had there been any other brand of useful knowledge, the possession of which could have been ascertained with equal precision, there was nothing to prevent its admission.'[11] He told the inspectorate that it was their job to make sure the curriculum was *not* narrowed down to an examination syllabus, and indeed insisted that inspection as well as examination be a condition for government funds, to ensure that 'the moral teaching, the discipline and the tone of the school were what they should be'.[12] Critics from Matthew Arnold downwards nonetheless insisted that, whatever Lowe's intentions, the system of pecuniary incentives he valued so highly would inevitably have the effect of aligning education with examination-passing in three subjects. Sylvester (1974), while discounting fantasies that a golden age of education had been developing until Lowe stamped on it, weighs the evidence carefully and pronounces the critics more right than wrong.

Opponents also complained – as they would about the publication of school league tables a century later – that school results depended as much on the location as on the quality of the school. It was this criticism which proved decisive. With most of the cabinet against him, Lowe was forced to assent to a compromise. Instead of the test and its required result depending on the child's age, it was to depend on its 'standard of accomplishment', this to be decided by the school itself.[13] The climbdown disgusted Lowe, and turned him into a reluctant friend of the teacher training colleges, whose certificates he now saw as the best remaining guarantor of adequate teaching. Shoring up this new enthusiasm for certification (he continued to oppose licensing, as has been seen), he reminded the Commons that even Adam Smith wanted to remove a seafarer's freedom to travel with a captain who could not navigate.[14]

This much was more or less dictated by the necessities of the situation; not so the heroic and heartening job description that followed.

> A school, like a church, is militant, continually fighting with innumerable foes – ignorance, vice and crime – which encompass it on every side. It may be compared with a luminous circle but its energies, though strained to the utmost, are often unable to make any impression upon the black mass around. Its work is never done; it is always beginning, never ending. Every child born in the world recruits the powers of ignorance, and you require all the inducements and stimulants that can possibly be applied in order to continue, with any hope of even partial success, what must be called a perpetual warfare.[15]

Many teachers, more accustomed to being used by Lowe to illustrate the principle of conservation of energy, must have rubbed their eyes as they read the parliamentary report. Matthew Arnold found it 'impossible to repress a smile'. But, as Winter (1976) points out, there is not even a psychological contradiction, let alone a logical one, between praising the ideal and recognising the human weaknesses that will probably get in its way.[16]

III

In 1864 Lowe resigned from the Board of Education after charges that school inspectors' reports had been unduly censored. In the end parliament exonerated him, but he stayed on the backbenches until moving to the Treasury in 1868. In the meantime the passage, against all Lowe's eloquence, of the 1867 Reform Act upturned his views on education.

> All the opinions I held on that subject are scattered to the winds by this measure of the Government... I believe it will be absolutely necessary that you should prevail on our future masters to learn their letters... I was opposed to centralisation, I am ready to accept centralisation; I was opposed to an education rate, I am ready now to accept it; I objected to inspection, I am now willing to create crowds of inspectors. The question is no longer a religious question, it has become a political one. It is indeed the question of questions; it has become paramount to every other question that has been brought before us. From the moment that you can intrust the masses with power their education becomes an absolute necessity, and our system of education... must give way to a national system.[17]

Lowe postponed a detailed discussion of the new educational necessities until November. Then, having told the Edinburgh Philosophical Institution that 'we must compel, and insist by some means that education shall become general in this country', he spelt out what the means should be. After standing by the Revised Code and proposing the compulsory inspection of all schools, Lowe came to his main proposal. Every parish without a voluntary school must be made to found a school of its own and support it. Compulsory education might be considered only when this had been done.[18]

The rest of Lowe's speech was about what schools should teach, not how pupils could be made to go and learn it. Furthermore, it was not wholly clear which of his remarks were aimed at, above or below the children of the country's 'new masters'. The poor, he said briefly at the end, had time so limited that we must fix upon very elementary modes of instruction. In general, however, the need was to learn about 'things not words... There must be speculation and there must be practice, but I think if we cannot do both we should rather lean to the practical part.'[19]

This sounds a considerable brake on social mobility. It was meant to be.

> The lower classes ought to be educated to discharge the duties cast upon them. They should also be educated that they may appreciate

> and defer to a higher cultivation when they meet it; and the higher classes ought to be educated in a very different manner, in order that they may exhibit to the lower classes that higher education to which, if it were shown to them, they would bow down and defer.[20]

Lowe tried to even things up by claiming a sense of inferiority when he met an intelligent workman, usually so much better educated in the things he needed to know than he, Lowe, was in his own curriculum. And Winter (1976) makes the justified point that the 'deference' Lowe wished to foster was not an ignorant self-abasement but a rational appreciation that some degree of inequality would benefit all. But it is hard to shrug off the understandable feeling of Lowe's twentieth-century educationist critics that, in unearthing this passage, they had struck gold.

The upper classes were not neglected in Lowe's Edinburgh speech. When he proceeded to enunciate a very long list of things an educated Englishman did not know but ought to, the target was Oxford graduates. One had just gained a First after his finals included an essay with 46 spelling mistakes, a second had gone on to be a political journalist despite never having heard of Lord Melbourne, a third visited France and would have died of starvation had the waiter not been better educated than he was.

Lowe's animus against his old university was already arousing pained comment there. He was unlikely to be able to resist making such remarks, and it certainly needed no Reform Bill to bring them forth. But the 1867 Act did also play a part in getting Lowe to rethink, or at least articulate more fully, his ideas on education for the middle class. That they had let the Bill through, that they had done nothing to resist their loss of power to the workers, showed up the defects in their education.

> I think I trace it to the want of common culture – I trace it to the want of something that should have raised men's minds to an attitude above the business of everyday cares, to make them take a more large, a more elevated, a more expanded view of their own position in society, in which they occupy so important a place.[21]

Instead, the middle classes were mostly getting '"technical education"' where children 'do at school precisely those things they would be called upon to do in after life'. This would not do: 'All knowledge almost, except heraldry, has some merits.'[22]

Lowe hoped that, even with heraldry excluded, this pronouncement would finally acquit him of the charge that 'I look upon education from a mean and sordid point of view, that I am for the education which enables a youth to get on in life and have no soul or apprehension for anything more.' In a touching passage, Lowe asked if anyone with his disabilities would be likely to take such a perspective:

> To a person like myself, excluded by physical causes from the more active pursuits and amusements of life, it is hardly possible to conceive the intense delight and happiness which reading gives. I should be the most ungrateful of mortals if I were not to say that learning has in itself charms which are infinitely better than the acquisition of money. All I can say is that had my eyes served me to become a close student you would not have seen me here today; no power could have drawn me from my books to the pursuits of an active life [cheers].[23]

And, far from feeling incompatibility between these sentiments and the Revised Code, Lowe believed that proper incentives for schools to teach the basics was the indispensable first step for children's induction into the world he had mastered with so much more pain than would be required of them, a view he reiterated four years later.

In 1872, Lowe had spent much of the summer in travelling round Scotland and collecting the freedom of one borough after another. In September he visited Anstruther to see the progress of its harbour, being rebuilt after two devastating storms. Because the cost included a subvention from the Treasury, Lowe characteristically refused the freedom of this particular borough, instead treating the townspeople to his latest thoughts on education.

> It was my duty, many years ago, to introduce what is called the Revised Code [A hiss]. Exactly, it was never popular with the schoolmasters, because it forces them to do exactly what they don't like – that is, to give their time mainly to the backward and

> more stupid children, instead of those who are more forward and promising. It was meant to do that and it did.

The Code, said Lowe, had also been of particular benefit to the children of the poor, whose parents 'are not always aware of the value of the education they reject for their children'.[24] This drew not a hiss but a cheer. Nor was it inconsistent with anything Lowe had said before. His belief that parents were the best judges of a good school presumed that they wanted a school in the first place. The state's duty came in when they did not. The point remains, however, that the state's duty had received little practical attention from Lowe until the 1867 Reform Act forced him to come down on its side.

Even Lowe's eventual rejection of the Revised Code did not, in his view, entail a reversal of principle. Asked by Lord George Hamilton whether he still stuck by the code, he replied, to Hamilton's amazement, 'If you will move for its total abolition in the House of Commons, I will second it.' Lowe still thought the Code right for the 'three R's'. But:

> the idiots who succeeded me have piled up on the top of the three R's a mass of class and specific subjects which they propose to test in the same way. The result is wholesale cramming and superficiality, for the great majority of children who pass through these class and specific subjects lose all knowledge of them a few months after they had left school.[25]

Readers familiar with Britain's educational reforms of the 1990s will already have been experiencing acute *déjà vu*. Now we find that the introduction of the national curriculum, followed by its disowning by its instigators after its three original subjects were inflated to thirteen, has a Victorian parallel too. The similarities become uncanny after Lowe's encomium on a 'Mr Woodhead' (presumably Nathaniel Woodard) who was setting up exactly the kind of schools for the middle class that he, Lowe, had been demanding.[26]

As Chancellor, Lowe played a major part in the 1870 Education Act. The Bill was very much in line with his own proposals of 1867–8. It made education neither free nor compulsory,[27] but compelled local authorities to set up a school in each parish where none existed. Such schools were to be funded by the rates, which immediately raised the dilemma of whether schools established by the various churches should get similar support. As they were relieving councils of the burden of starting their own schools, it seemed they should. But the political difficulty of getting ratepayers to subsidise religions they might detest seemed insuperable. The solution came from Lowe. It was his suggestion that public funds for denominational schools come from central, not local, government that finally aligned critics in Gladstone's cabinet behind the Act.

To Lowe the Act was a settlement of the education question in line with the needs of democracy. His relative silence on educational matters in the 1870s is therefore unsurprising. There was, however, a renewed emphasis on pedagogy as a mere preliminary to the real business of education, teaching yourself. Lowe told the Halifax Mechanics Institution that schools should not cram a pupil with information he might easily acquire himself, but rather impart 'a facile command of the means of, in after life, gaining knowledge for himself'.[28] Mechanics considering self-instruction were pointed in the direction of *The Wealth of Nations*. By 1879 Lowe was going further, earning the cheers of students at Croydon School of Art when he assured them that there was nothing in the world more overvalued than teaching. 'What a man could be taught by another was as nothing compared to what he could teach himself.'[29]

IV

Especially at the universities, whose lazy and incompetent teachers seemed set to reign for ever. The exception was Lowe's own constituency, the University of London. Until his election here (in place of Calne) in 1868, Lowe had tended to lump all universities together, criticising the content of degree courses as well as the standard of teaching. Like Smith, he saw endowment as the curse of higher education, but partly because of its distortion of the curriculum. A young man with a First in classics might be fellow of half-a-dozen Oxford colleges; his counterpart in physics would be lucky to secure a berth at all. Small wonder, said Lowe, that Oxford at any rate was incapable of reforming itself.[30]

Lowe had been highly unimpressed by the reforms in the 1854 Universities Act, particularly when it failed to incorporate his liberalising measure that any member of Oxford's convocation might take in undergraduates and set up as a hall of residence. But his attack on Oxford intensified once he was elected for London in 1868. In his speech of thanks to the electors (London graduates) he assured them that their degrees were a greater achievement, and hence a greater honour, than the Oxbridge equivalent. If they wanted a knowledgeable assessment of the Oxford pass degree, they should consult the Dean of Christ Church, who had just pronounced it 'quite worthless'. After a swipe at the MPs for Oxford University, or its dons, or both ('If you want to know what the men who live in Oxford think... take the reverse of the opinions of her representatives in Parliament'), Lowe rhetorically asked how London had attained a position of which any other university might be envious. The answer was simple. Teaching was separated from examination: until this was done there was a motive 'to lower the examination to the requirements of the teaching'.[31] This was what went on at Oxford and Cambridge, which places might like to reflect that a man did not normally audit his own accounts, and where the leniency at examination time was 'perfectly inconceivable'.[32] Indeed it was time that these universities – and everyone else – realised that teaching and examination should not just be in different hands but required wholly opposite principles. The former was an occupation where you could not have too much competition, the latter a judicial process where you could not have too little.[33]

Oxford met Lowe's barbs with a dignified silence. The dons – a larger and more confident breed than those who judged Mrs Thatcher in 1985 – even gave him an honorary degree, gilding the honour with a citation defining him as 'frugalissimus'. Lowe 'was delighted and joined in the shout of laughter'.[34] It did not stanch his invective, which rose in pitch until he finally drew blood. When he told parliament that Oxford undergraduates 'might spend their time in idleness and yet pass the examination', Thomas Fowler of Lincoln College retorted that only one student in five was taking a pass degree; the rest were up for honours. That proved nothing, said Lowe: in some subjects honours were easier to obtain than a pass. 'In the lowest depths the University has found a lower deep.' That, said Fowler, was an accusation of fraud. 'But I cannot help feeling that no arguments and no statement of facts will avail against the inveterate prejudice which Mr Lowe for some suitable reason has conceived against his university.'[35]

Given Lowe's reticence as to the source of his judgements, Fowler may well have had a point. But if Lowe was in fact using *a priori* deduction as a substitute for fact, his starting point remained unchanged and, as far as Oxford dons went, unchallenged. Only external examination could provide any kind of standard. On these grounds Lowe was shortly to oppose independent status for Owens College, Manchester, whose examinations were currently set by London. Once students were taught *and* examined by a so-called University of Manchester, said Lowe, it would quickly sink to Oxbridge standards.[36]

V

If the divorce of teaching and testing could not be arranged, there remained one last hope for the universities – the consequences of Lowe's own civil service reform of 1870. As this reform was arguably his greatest achievement, it must be stressed from the start that no one, least of all Lowe himself, saw the implications for higher education as anything more than a by-product, albeit an important one.

The Northcote–Trevelyan reforms (1854) had stopped well short of a civil service recruited by examination. The new Civil Service Commission was set up to hold examinations, but the principle was to be certification not licensing: no department had to choose successful examinees. As Chancellor after 1870 Lowe enforced such compulsion on all departments except the Home Office (which he brought into line in 1873 by the device of moving there himself) and the Foreign Office. The means was not an Act of parliament but an Order in Council giving the Treasury control over recruitment procedures.

The democratic dangers of the age had turned Lowe into a middle-aged man in a hurry to build a citadel of educated intellect at the heart of public affairs: a citadel, indeed, that would inspire education in the same measure as it drew upon it. Candidates for the higher ranks of the civil service were already being examined in a syllabus close enough to what Oxford and Cambridge offered to involve these universities in the practical pursuit of their students' ambitions, yet distinct enough to put some pressure on them to modernise their curricula. It was Lowe's hope that the 1870 Order in Council would greatly enhance this pressure. The enthusiastic support of Benjamin Jowett, Master of Balliol (the administrators' college *par excellence*) and an old friend of Lowe's, was the happiest of omens. For entry to lesser posts, the Treasury instituted a simpler examination, suited to, but again suited to prod, the elementary and technical schools. The spur to the universities was to be mirrored at one level down: more suitable curricula *and* more demand for education in the light of the new rewards at the end of it.[37]

With characteristic tact, Lowe treated the civil service to a speech in which he looked forward to the day when competitive examination had rid the government of all its 'overpaid and incapable clerks'.[38] However, he opposed competitions for promotion *within* the civil service, insisting that this should continue to be done on the nomination of superiors. Clerks applying to rise above clerical rank, for example, might succeed in an examination despite being unsuitable. What if, in their unaccustomed contact with the upper class, they found themselves overawed and unable to hold their own?[39]

The solution to the problem would have been generous provision of state scholarships to the public schools and universities. Winter (1976) picks out as critical the fact that this option apparently never occurred to Lowe: his failure to consider it, Professor Winter claims, conclusively settles his order of priorities as anti-statism first, careers open to talent second. The trouble with this interpretation is that within five years Lowe *was* proposing extensive state assistance to poor pupils. The government, he said, should offer

> such prizes and endowments as would induce parents to send their children to [secondary schools] . . . They should then have an examination for young men, and Government should be willing to supply very liberally funds and rewards for those students who might have shown fair proficiency in their examinations, so that by scholarships they should act with equal liberality and give those young men, who showed that they had acquired a sufficient mastery of the subjects in which they were examined, exhibitions, or something of the kind, lasting for seven or eight years, which would enable such young men to get a fair start in life.[40]

Keeping students on public money until their thirtieth year is hardly sacrificing poor boys' chances to classical liberalism. It must be stressed that Lowe made this speech long after his ministerial career was over: also that he was speaking specifically about Ireland. However, those wanting to do inductive logic on Lowe pronouncements can normally transport him, bag and baggage and in perfect safety, from one side of the Irish Sea to the other. That was his own boast – and his critics' complaint – as will be seen in Chapter 6.

VI

On higher education, Lowe was less radical than Smith. He stopped short of calling for lecturers to be paid at the classroom door – though his advice to undergraduates to seek a private tutor and take little notice of other instructions on offer comes to much the same thing. But his views on the universities are in any case less important than what he said, and did, about schools. The second Reform Bill may have been the trigger to his about-turn in 1867. But the real interest of the episode is its picture of an old-fashioned utilitarian coming to terms with the increased power of the nineteenth-century state.

In this respect the years from 1865 to 1868 were the climacteric of Lowe's intellectual career. On no less than four of the leading questions of the day – the franchise, education, Ireland and the trades unions – he had to make up his mind whether to stay with his existing ideal of a government chosen by an elite cadre of voters, operating a minimal state apparatus and brooking no interference with freedom of contract. On none of the other three issues did he undergo a reversal comparable with education. What he decided to do on each is the theme of the next three chapters.

5
Shedding Daylight on the Unions

In 1867 Lowe told his brother that he was writing an article for the *Quarterly Review* on the trades unions which would 'shed some daylight on those august institutions'.[1] It shed at least as much light on its author.

Lowe was turning his attention to the unions just as they were acquiring a new rationale from the decline of the wage-fund theory. This doctrine had been so named because it posited a fund which had to be paid out to support labour before it could produce goods and services. In a largely agrarian society where a worker's main consumption was of food, and where the harvest was inexorably annual, it was an unsurprising doctrine for economists to adopt. The wage fund *was* in essence the harvest, and the implication followed naturally that a higher wage for one group of workers must involve a lower wage or (through unemployment) no wage for others.

Even industrialisation and the increasing consumption of industrial goods by the workers themselves left the theory largely intact for many years. While historians of economic thought have rightly pointed to a wide variety of interpretations of the fund, at least by the middle of the nineteenth century, John Stuart Mill remained sufficiently convinced both to state it in its traditional form through the first six editions of his *Principles of Political Economy* and, when Thornton attacked it head-on in 1869, to recant rather than take refuge in the vagueness the theory had acquired in some other hands. Coming from Mill, the recantation sounded very like an official obituary.

The employer, said Mill, had no fixed fund for the exclusive payment of wages.

> That fund is co-extensive with the whole proceeds of his business, after keeping up his machinery, buildings or materials and feeding his family; and it is expanded jointly upon himself and his labourers... The real limit to the rise [in wages] is the practical consideration, how much would ruin him, or drive him to abandon his business: not the inexorable limit of the wage fund.[2]

Lowe was not alone in ignoring Mill's recantation. As Biagini (1987) has shown, some of the worst diehards were trade unionists, a few of whom were still invoking the wage fund in its original glory down to the end of the 1870s. But as the wage fund tottered in the late 1860s, Lowe preferred to reflect on whether the repeal of the Combination Acts in 1825 had actually legalised trade unions. The unions, he said, had no power unless members agreed to be bound by the will of the majority. But such agreement was probably illegal given that a court had recently ruled this in the case of employers' federations. Symmetry between the two sides of industry was a lifelong part of Lowe's creed, normatively and positively, and not least in terms of their bargaining powers. The unions might have persuaded themselves that the capitalist could take or leave the labourer, while the worker was at his employer's mercy. The reality was rather different; indeed the worker, who could take his labour where he wished, had advantages over the employer, whose capital could not be removed and must stand idle if he could not find labour.[3] And, whereas once 'the master dealt with the labourer as man with man, and each entered into and put an end to the contract according to his own goodwill and pleasure',[4] now the worker, by agreeing to submit to union majority rulings or be expelled, 'sells himself into slavery'.[5]

What advantage did the worker get in return? The *objective*, said Lowe, was to get as much out of the wage fund as possible, and was pursued without thought of where that fund came from, what were the conditions necessary to its continuance, or what a higher wage would do to employment. As for strikes, they simply reduced wages. Wages depended on demand for labour which was in turn given by the rate of profit. Where an industry's profits were high, it would attract entrants, bidding for the workers and pushing up the wage;

a strike threatened all this. Where profits were low, strikes just drove capital out of the trade. These strikes did not have to be about wages as such. Any strike, on any grievance, was 'bullying' of employers which would either dry up the demand for labour or make employers require *higher* profits (i.e. lower wages) to make it worth their while to stay in business.[6]

How could the unions fail to see all this? asked Lowe. Even they had finally had to recognise that protection and Luddism had damaged the working class: yet 'trades unions one and all seem utterly reckless of the degree in which they increase the expenses of production'. Like every other critic of the unions over the last 200 years, Lowe thought they should learn some economics. But instead the unions struck or threatened to strike in accordance with a 'political economy' based on two principles: that the wage fund was inexhaustible and that the actual level of wages was determined by the level of capitalist greed.[7]

An exception, said Lowe, was the London Trades Council, which had finally discovered that excessive wage demands repelled capital and ended up lowering the actual wage. But their remedy, Lowe reported with horror, was to go global. They had resolved that the condition of the working class would never improve while 'the people of different countries have no regular intercommunication among themselves for the purpose of regulating the hours of labour and assimilating wages'. Lowe wasted little time on this 'attempt to overrule the laws of nature' which would merely substitute international for national unemployment. Unions should indeed think globally, but would be better occupied in supporting freer migration of labour around the world. But the working class had always been strongly against competition from immigrants. In any case, Lowe admitted, immigration would help the British worker only by the doubtless unwelcome route of competing wages downward and thus improving Britain's competitive position. To improve employment *and* wages, the question was how to improve competition for labour among employers.[8]

Just as damaging as striking for higher wages were unions' demands that all workers be paid the same. This too was founded on misunderstood economics. Instead of realising that remuneration was adapted to skill, trades unionists saw wages as 'more in the nature of the spoils of a civil war'. This being so, it was unsurprising that they wanted the spoils divided equally. If the wage fund were seen as a prize for which all had fought in unison, no wonder they felt it 'ought not to be encroached on by the superior strength and dexterity of a few'.[9] In Lowe's peroration all restraint left him:

> We say that [unions] injure in the most vital manner the interest of the very working class whom they are meant to aid, that they threaten some branches of manufactures with extinction and seriously limit the diffusion of others, that they are carried on by means fatal to every right that a free country respects, that they are ruinous to the legitimate ambitions of industry and merit, that they can only be conducted by a systematic breach of the law, that they run through the whole gamut of crime, from a mere conspiracy in restraint of trade, to robbery, arson, mutilation and murder.[10]

II

This was written against the background of the 'Sheffield Outrages' of the 1860s. The Sheffield saw-grinders had a simple course of treatment for anyone who fell behind with their union dues, employed too many apprentices, or entered the trade without their approval. They sabotaged his equipment and, if that failed, threatened his life. After the second death a royal commission was set up. At the same time the Hornby *v.* Close judgment of 1867 had, *pace* Lowe, questioned the unions' legality. Ruling that a union could not sue an embezzling official, the court justified this by arguing that their 'restraint of trade' undercut the unions' legal status.

Thus, on entering office in 1868, Gladstone's ministry faced the demands both of anti-unionists who thought the criminal law had been too lax and of unionists concerned that the civil law was eating away at the concessions they had won since the repeal of the Combination Acts in 1825. The unions' fears did not rest on Hornby *v.* Close alone. In 1867 the Conservatives had amended the long-standing Master and Servant Act, ostensibly in the direction of putting employers and workers on a more equal legal footing. The result in practice, however, was that workers who broke their contracts continued to face criminal charges while employers who did the same could only be sued.

Gladstone left the Master and Servant Act alone. But a pair of Acts passed in 1871 tried to deal with the other issues. The Trade Union Act provided that 'restraint of trade' no longer be grounds for charges of conspiracy, but its twin, the Criminal Law Amendment Act, reiterated the criminality of 'coercion', 'intimidation' and 'molestation'. The issue was now what forms of picketing were legal. First, the House of Lords amended the Act to make even a solitary picket an offence. Then the Gas Stokers' Case of December 1872 revealed that, in the hands of a determined judge, the Trade Union Act had *not* exempted striking unions from conspiracy charges.

As Chancellor, Lowe stayed aloof from all this. But, within a few days of becoming Home Secretary in August 1873, he was challenging the wisdom not only of the Tories' Master and Servant Act (1867) but also of his own government's Criminal Law Amendment Act (1871).[11] The 1867 Bill, with criminal penalties for workers, but not for employers, who broke their contracts, was, Lowe said, class legislation at its most inflammatory. As for the 1871 Act, it had effectively outlawed picketing.

Gladstone issued his standard 'have another look at it and then do something if you like' reply, kept on hand for occasions of particular indifference.[12] But when Lowe sent him a long memorandum with proposals for addressing the unions' grievances, Gladstone had it printed and circulated to the rest of the cabinet. Essentially, Lowe's proposals would have got rid of any special laws which, in intention or in practice, singled out the unions for punitive treatment. The law against conspiracy would exclude conspiracies to commit acts not criminal in themselves, or acts minor enough to come before a mere magistrate. The Master and Servant Act should go altogether:

> It would be very impolitic now that attention has been drawn to this act, to enter into a contest with the working classes in a matter in which they appear to be absolutely right. I hold that there is no sound distinction between contracts to buy and sell labour and contracts to buy and sell any other commodity, and the sooner this absolute equality between all persons contracting irrespective of the subject matter of the contract is recognised, the better.[13]

The cabinet accepted most of this but was out of office before anything could be done. The incoming Tories refused to act immediately and set up another Royal Commission, which ended up in broad agreement with Lowe's proposals. But Lowe himself had now moved on and no longer thought this enough. Now he pressed his successor at the Home Office, R.A. Cross, to make picketing a fully legal activity. Many MPs of both parties had decided the time had come to do this and, with Lowe placing himself at their head, they won through.[14]

Lowe now moved on to industrial accidents. Chairing a select committee on employment law in 1877, he asked it to recommend that the employer be held liable whenever a worker was injured through a fellow-worker's negligence. In that way, said Lowe, the worker could sue someone who might actually be able to pay up. The committee overruled its chairman, recommending the owners be liable for the negligence only of those they had delegated to manage.[15] Lowe refrained from bringing about a minority report, but made it clear in the subsequent Commons debate that Disraeli's government was itself negligent of the interest of the working man.[16]

But how far had Lowe's position really changed between the 1860s and 1870s? Opposition to what he saw as class legislation was a consistent, passionate and fundamental theme of his career, dating back to his fight with the Australian squatters in the 1840s. Nor, unlike many liberals, did he accommodate a leftward (or rightward) journey with elastic criteria of what counted as class legislation. That the 1867 *Quarterly Review* article was a protest against excessive power for any section of the economy, not just the workers, was revealed in Lowe's brief but graphic description of the consequences of a privileged alliance between labour and capital. As for employer liability, Lowe would have seen nothing inconsistent in supporting workplace rights but opposing trade unionism.

The one fact which cannot be explained away in this fashion is Lowe's later stand on picketing. Mellowing out of office and in one's mid-sixties is one thing but accusing both parties of being too harsh on yesterday's robbers, arsonists, mutilators and murderers is another. Winter (1976) convincingly locates the rationale for Lowe's change of heart in a speech he made in 1872. Whereas Lowe (at any rate as an economist) had previously made little or no distinction between social classes and special interest groups, he now looked forward to a future where the former might break down into the latter, removing the threat of class war and socialism. The best help that governments could give this process was to do nothing that unnecessarily kept class resentments alive.[17]

That the unions offended the principles of free trade was too obvious to Lowe to need much labouring. Less predictable was a passage in the *Quarterly Review* article where he argued that the existence of unionism may be a reason for limiting free trade. Unless 'freedom of production' were restored, he said, 'we must modify the freedom of trade to suit the fettered and weakened state of production . . . you cannot be all *laissez faire* on one side and all regulation and interference on the other.'[18]

Why not? Lowe presumably had in mind that trade union 'fetters' made it harder for industry to compete abroad. Yet, contemporary with the *Quarterly Review* article, leader after leader in *The Times* was taking to task anyone who dared suggest that victims of protection ought to impose some of their own. Lowe was quite clear about the Ricardian case against doing this. But how can protection be no remedy for burdens imposed by others yet efficacious when the burdens are self-imposed? Lowe never explained.

6
What Shall We Do for Ireland?

Lowe had shown his anti-relativist leanings early in his career, when in 1853 he turned in a minority report on Indian law reform. The majority of the parliamentary commission (set up under the 1853 India Act) had insisted on tailoring Indian laws to the specific needs and traditions of the different states. Unnecessary, said Lowe: English law was already in force across much of India, and the commission should save its time by bringing the remaining districts into line. But Lowe's best-known assault on relativism was incidental to the Irish question.

Whereas Nassau Senior had addressed Ireland's problems by hoping for a modern capitalist system of agriculture, Lowe, in the 1860s, was confident these hopes were at last coming true. Thus from the start he was in collision with Mill, who had reacted to the potato famine by opening his long campaign to keep the peasants on the land with security of tenure, or compensation for improvements they had made as tenants, or both. Capitalist farming, Mill said in 1847, was 'wholly impracticable . . . the people are there, and the problem is not to improve the country but to see how it can be improved by and for its present inhabitants'.[1] These sentiments, incorporated the following year into Mill's *Principles of Political Economy*, framed Mill's successive policy proposals for the rest of his life.[2]

Parliament since 1836 had been considering and rejecting private members' bills to compensate evicted Irish tenants for improvements. One such bill was even introduced by Peel's government but dropped when it became clear it would not get through the Lords. The succeeding Russell administration tried to go down Mill's and

Senior's roads simultaneously. By passing the 1849 Incumbered Estates Act, which made the sale of mortgaged land easier, it hoped that *both* sitting tenants *and* large-scale capitalist farmers would take advantage. The results were disappointing on both counts. Cardwell's Act of 1860 gave tenants compensation for some varieties of improvement, but only with the landlord's consent and only for future improvements, not existing ones.

Lowe entered the debate just as his uncompromising views were going out of fashion on the Liberal and Conservative front benches. Palmerston, to whom fixity of tenure was 'communistic' and tenant's right 'equivalent to landlord's wrong'[3] had been dead a matter of months when Chichester Fortescue, now Irish Chief Secretary, introduced a bill which would compensate any tenant on a lease of under 31 years for improvements he made. The Bill fell with the Liberal government, but not before Lowe, on 17 May 1866, had invited his opponents to put up a relativist case for the proposal. If, he said, it was being advanced in grounds peculiar to Ireland, 'I can understand it. But if the ground is that of natural justice and right, it is not peculiar to one side of the Channel or the other.'[4] At this stage, then, the absolute nature of the laws of political economy was not the issue.

The critical fact, Lowe told parliament, was that the existing system was beginning to work. In his very proposal of the Bill the Chief Secretary for Ireland had 'stated in the most glowing manner the wonderful improvements which had been going on in Ireland since 1841'.[5] Nor had he claimed that the existing law would prevent similar improvements in the future. Why, then, the Bill?

Replying directly to Lowe, Mill asserted that the Bill *did* rest on grounds peculiar to Ireland. The point was not that England and Ireland were currently under the same legal system, but that they were experiencing very different results within its framework. In England tenants and landlords mostly trusted each other. Improvements were often planned together and, even if not, the tenant did not fear that the landlord would appropriate their value to himself. In Ireland, by contrast, there was 'no confidence at all between landlords and tenants'.[6]

But Mill was equally ready to take on Lowe on natural justice and right. What, after all, he asked, underlay the *landlord*'s right to his land? The fact that someone had once improved it. Mere appropriation of common land with nothing invested in it would *not* generally be seen as furnishing a right to own it in perpetuity. 'Unless we recognise on the same ground a kindred claim in the temporary occupier', Mill concluded 'we give up the moral basis on which landed property rests'.[7]

While Lowe made no direct reply to these arguments, he kept the issue very much alive in a series of *Times* leaders over the next two years (during which time the Conservatives introduced a much weaker version of Fortescue's bill and failed to enact even that). And in 1868 the *Quarterly Review* published his most extended contribution on the subject, 'What Shall We Do for Ireland?'

Here a more authentic Robert Lowe pushed aside the fairly mild parliamentarian of the past two years. Ireland, he said, had two kinds of land tenure, 'the one regulated by law, the creature of contract, exactly similar to the tenure of England: the other regulated by secret societies and enforced by the bludgeon and the blunderbuss'.[8] The tenant taking over improvements from a predecessor would speedily discover the reach of the second system, the compensation he would have to pay being

> a kind of tribute or blackmail ... in order to purchase a quiet enjoyment of his holding, in order, in fact, that he may not be shot from behind a hedge as he returns from market, or find a grave amid the burning rafters of his own farmhouse.[9]

Meanwhile 'the natural answer of a landlord to a tenant-at-will seeking to enforce compensation for improvements would be a notice to quit'. The response of reformers, in turn, would be that tenure must in that case be made more secure. Fixity of tenure would involve a quit rent which in time would also be declared an intolerable burden. In this way would the land 'be wrested from its present owners and return to the Celtic race again'.[10]

But even before this final stage, fixed tenure would fix Irish agriculture in its current inept state – at best. Even compensation for improvements, let alone its inevitable consequents, would entrench the evil of too-small holdings with too many people on them, generally clamouring for subdivision so as to make everything even more hopeless. Compensation for improvement would

> put into action a set of causes which must infallibly drag Ireland down to the fearful position she held before 1846. You will give her back her lost millions, to be swept away by another famine.[11]

If the small tenant was a problem, so was the small landlord, especially the kind who would burgeon under Mill's proposal to advance money to tenants to buy existing landlords out:

> Who deal more hardly with the tenant, the rich proprietors who have inherited the land, or the small capitalists who buy it for an investment, determined to wring every shilling out of it and to use to the utmost the power over their tenants which the unnatural demand for the occupation of land puts at their disposal?[12]

Mill, who had used the independent peasant proprietor to idealise his vision of 'the stationary state', and who had now progressed to demanding the nationalisation of Irish land, was quick in rebuttal. Lowe was predicting for Ireland exactly the disaster that peasant proprietorship had supposedly been going to bring about in France. And yet what was happening there? A falling rural population – despite inheritance laws far more unpromising than Ireland's – and a rising standard of living as peasants realised that hard work now led to something other than an increased rent.[13]

Lowe remained unconvinced: all Mill's remedies were bad ones in his eyes. And this was because Mill had mistaken the problem. The system of land tenure was not at the root of Ireland's difficulties. So what, in Lowe's opinion, was?

Lowe's two main exercises in diagnosis were a parliamentary speech of February 1865, and the 1868 article 'What Shall We Do for Ireland?' that we have just been considering. Putting them side by side is instructive. For, while both locate the problem and the solution alike with the Irish people and not the British government, the accusations in the 1868 article are more extensive and many times more strident.

In particular, Lowe changed his mind about why Ireland was short of capital. In 1865 he had refused to blame it on the 'unhappy discords and divisions in Ireland'. Other countries had been 'torn by the most dreadful contests' – South Africa, the USA, even England in former days – but accumulation had continued. Nor was capital repelled by the intrinsic characteristics of the Irish, who prospered well enough in Australia.[14] Yet by 1868 it was 'the peculiarities of the Irish character' and 'the national genius for conspiracy and combination' which 'banish manufactures and commerce from her shores'.[15]

No doubt it was the Fenian rising of 1865–7, particularly its atrocities on the British mainland, which caused at least part of Lowe's change of attitude.[16] In one respect he continued to agree with Mill's analysis. Land laws the same as England's had very different results in Ireland because of the enfeebled bargaining position of the tenantry: their demand for land was so strong that the landlord could do what he pleased. But from this Lowe drew two lessons contrary to Mill. The first was that landholding could not be regulated by law but depended 'on economical conditions and the state of society in the country'.[17] This was why, for example, no large estates existed in the USA; labour was so expensive that no one wanted wage-earners and land so plentiful that no one needed to be a tenant. Lowe, in short, was arguing that the relativism of economic systems *reduced* the rationale for relativist legislation. But the other lesson Lowe drew was specific to Ireland. If the tenant's plight was caused by his insatiable demand for land, the only cure was to reduce it, and this could be done only by finding alternative employment for some would-be tenants. If it were the discordant behaviour of the Irish repelling manufactures, the remedy was in their hands: if they refused to take it, the only solution left was emigration.

At this point Lowe reminded his readers that not all the troubles of the Irish were their own fault. It was a complex of historical and natural forces which had brought them 'to depend entirely upon agriculture in a country with a humid and uncertain climate and a not very grateful soil'.[18] In 1865 he had analysed these forces at length. Ireland's worst misfortune had been the Corn Laws, which, by encouraging cereals in a moist climate 'fit principally for pasturing cattle', had made the Irish people dependent on an industry which rose and fell with their capricious weather. When England came to its senses at last and repealed the Corn Laws, it was too late: Irish farmers (like many English ones) were set in their pattern and 'clung to cereal and potato production instead of raising stock'.[19] It was inevitable and desirable that Ireland should eventually transform itself into a pastoral country: but now this was finally happening, labour was bound to be displaced. With no manufacturing to go to, emigration was inevitable:

> I can imagine no condition more irritating, depressing or discouraging than that. It is deserving of our utmost sympathy and compassion, and, if it be in our power, of alleviation: but, unhappily, that is beyond our power.[20]

Once again, by 1868 the tone had changed, melancholia swept away by brisk accusation:

> It has been the pleasure of Ireland to pass upon herself a sentence of perpetual poverty. She drives away manufactures by strikes; she frightens away capital by agrarian outrage. While she denounces absenteeism, she makes the position of a resident proprietor almost intolerable.[21]

What with this *and* the high birthrate emigration was 'almost the only possible relief' for unemployment.

> Mr Gladstone has undertaken to check it. He will not succeed, but if he did he would do Ireland the greatest injury imaginable and destroy the only palliative for her misfortunes.[22]

Lowe consistently ignored Gladstone's well-founded point that emigration from Ireland was emigration of the most capable, the most enterprising and those most needed to put Ireland on the road to prosperity. Nor did Lowe's remarks about peasants 'clinging' to potato farming reveal much understanding of the plight of a class largely too poor to invest in change, and often without any kind of capital equipment except a spade for digging up potatoes. But, to Lowe, it was Gladstone and Mill who condemned Ireland to an unnecessarily dismal future. While Mill was right to portray the poverty of the Irish tenant farmer

> We are asked ... to concede that this miserable condition of affairs is the be-all and end-all of that country ... They say we must accept this as the ultimate stage of civilisation to which Ireland

can aspire, and that we must take every means in our power to stereotype and perpetuate it.[23]

II

That was in March 1868. By the end of the year Lowe was in government with Gladstone, a government, moreover, whose mission was 'to pacify Ireland'. Gladstone's first task was to disestablish the Irish Church (whereupon Lowe told a Liberal meeting that, while other governments had talked about justice to Ireland, Gladstone had done it).[24] But after that Gladstone lost little time in submitting the outline of an Irish Land Bill to his cabinet. Tenants would get government loans to help them buy the land they farmed. They would have compensation if evicted 'arbitrarily' from their plots or forced out by 'excessive' rent increases; and tenants evicted for any reason would be compensated for improvements they had made. Predictably, Lowe condemned the proposal as

> a direct attack on property, a direct breach of the duty of the government to do impartial justice between all its subjects, a precedent under which any amount of spoliation ought as far as principle goes to be justified, the fining of one class for the benefit of another, the transfer of money from one man to another without fault in the person amerced or merit in the person enriched, the forcing of new and arbitrary terms into existing contracts, the breaking of faith pledged to the purchasers in the encumbered estates Court and the undermining of all confidence in the justice and courage of the Government.[25]

And all this for a measure which was most unlikely to conciliate tenants, who would now find themselves 'placed under a veto of the landlord as to improvements'.

Lowe's position throughout 1869 was that Gladstone's proposals threw away too many principles for too little practical help to the Irish tenant. Indeed, by 'raising a storm', they had ratcheted up the help which would now have to be given without doing anything useful to give it.[26] The government thus needed to find an immediate way of conciliating the Irish peasantry without sacrificing the permanent principles on which land ownership rightly rested and which 'will become every day better suited to Ireland as she improves'.[27] A way must be found to retain the existing law of contract, yet suspend the practice of leaving everything to it.

Lowe therefore came up with the idea of 'Courts of Conscience and Conciliation', to decide disputes between landlord and tenant not on any fixed rules of procedure but on 'the principles of equity, used in its moral and not in its Chancery sense'. Because the Courts were to be a temporary expedient, they would not 'shake the foundation of property'; because they would not be limited to compensating evictions or improvements but 'range over the whole relation of landlord and tenant', they would pacify Ireland better than anything Gladstone had proposed. These courts, said Lowe, 'should be guided simply by the consideration of what is fair and just between man and man'.[28] When Gladstone commented that discretion of this purity would place landlord and tenant alike at the mercy of 'third rate Irish lawyers', Lowe wondered if it might not be possible to furnish the Courts with 'some good moral ideas, which without being exactly truisms or copy book maxims should yet be more general and more plastic than the rules of positive law'.[29]

In the end Gladstone persuaded Lowe to support a compromise Bill which specifically denied compensation to tenants evicted for non-payment of rent, and allowed the landlord to extend any tenant's lease to 31 years in order to escape claims for compensation.[30] Outside cabinet, with no negotiations to conduct or compromises to steer, Lowe remained closer to his underlying instincts. On the same day as he proposed the Compensation Courts he told Lady Salisbury that he had never been able to understand 'the grievance of holding people to their contracts, nor able to find a better plan than leaving every man to do as he likes with his own time and labour'.[31] The charge against Lowe, stretching from Mill (1868) through Leslie (1879) to Moore (1996) was that he had shut himself off from such understanding by his conception of political economy. In a passage well known to historians of economic thought, Mill, speaking in parliament on 12 March 1868, declared 'Political economy has many enemies, but its worst enemies are some of its friends, and I do not know that it has a more dangerous enemy than my hon. Friend.'[32] Lowe, said Mill, had spoken 'as if science was a thing not to guide our judgement, but to stand in its place.[33] But:

> so far from being a set of maxims and rules to be applied without regard to times, places and circumstances, the function of political economy is to enable us to find the rules to govern any state of circumstances with which we have to deal ... it does not supply us with a ready-made judgement upon any case, and there cannot be a greater enemy to political economy than he who represents it in that light.[34]

Mill may or may not have felt these strictures described Lowe's economics in general: he was specifically criticising the speech Lowe had made immediately before his own. In this speech Lowe had pressed the laws of economics into the service of one thing only – freedom to dispose of your property as you wish

> there is an oasis in the desert of politics upon which we may safely rest, and that is afforded by the principles of political economy. In accordance with the best ascertained principles of political economy, as well as of law, every man who has made money is entitled to invest it in land; and if you introduce arbitrary restrictions with respect to land, you artificially depreciate that description of property compared with other property. Freedom of disposition of land is a strong stimulus to that desire of accumulation on which the wealth of nations depend. I entertain a prejudice derived from Scotland and adopted by Adam Smith, that a man is at liberty to do what he likes with his own, and that having land, it is not unreasonable that he should be free to let his land to a person of full age upon the terms upon which they shall mutually agree. That I believe to be reason and good political economy.[35]

One reason why political economy could bring to Ireland this sole – if supremely important – lesson was that Lowe, as has been seen, excluded so much from the subject's scope.

> The questions so much agitated by Mr Mill, as to whether small cultivation is better than large, are not political; no, nor, with all deference to him be it said, are they politico-economical: they belong to the science of practical agriculture, and to the practical agriculturist we should leave them to work out for himself.[36]

Even Lowe could hardly have expected Mill to be warned off the question on the strength of this, and in 1870 Mill, in 'Leslie and the Land Question', returned to the attack on economists who

> believe themselves to be provided with a set of catch-words, which they mistake for principles – free trade, freedom of contract, competition, demand and supply, the wages fund, individual interest, desire of wealth, &c. – which supersede analysis, and are applicable to every variety of cases without the trouble of thought.[37]

Perhaps this is aimed specifically at Lowe – Mill does not say. But does Lowe deserve it? We have seen little evidence of his using free trade or any other of the phrases on Mill's list as a substitute for analysis. The one 'catchword' he did use to try and close arguments down was not the name of some topic in political economy but the name of political economy itself. And even here it is sparingly invoked. Precisely because Lowe does use it as a slogan, it in the end adds nothing essential to the edifice of his arguments over Ireland – an edifice which would look very little different had Lowe never referred to the scope, nature or methodology of economics in his life.

III

And while Mill (now no longer in parliament) was examining Leslie and the land question, a startled Commons heard Lowe dispense, not with discourse about political economy, but with political economy itself. The Irish land Bill had now reached the committee stage. There is no apparent reason why Lowe, as Chancellor, should have put himself up as its chief defender. When he did, MPs were divided whether he had adequately answered his own speeches of 1867–8, but were unanimous that they had witnessed a particularly brazen volte-face.

Lowe began by denying that the Bill compromised the principle of free disposal of property. It did not remove the right to evict a tenant. 'The disturbance of a tenant by eviction is a legal act, and a man is right in doing it.' But:

> it is a right the exercise of which is particularly liable to abuse . . . it is a right which ought to be exercised with great care, discretion, kindness and moderation, because if it be wrongly exercised, it is

> a calamity not only to the tenant, not only, as frequently happens in Ireland, to the parties that execute that right, but also to the neighbourhood, the county, the country, and the Empire at large.[38]

To impose fines on landlords who evicted their tenants would have infringed their rights. Instead the government was proposing compensation – to be decided in each case on its merits – when a landlord exercised his right to evict improperly.

As compensation was all that had ever been proposed, Lowe's lawyerly distinction did not help him establish his own consistency between 1868 and 1870. But he soldiered on. Eviction in Ireland, he said, was invariably a catastrophe for the tenant, given the pressure on land and his meagre chances of finding another holding. English tenants did not need the protection being offered to Ireland.

The exceptionally weak bargaining position of the Irish peasant was, as we have seen, a constant refrain of Lowe's. Nonetheless, as his speech neared its end, he had to all appearances buried both his doctrine that political economy enjoined freedom to dispose of your own property as you pleased, and his proclamation that good political economy for England could not be bad political economy for Ireland. Lowe took the only route that remained open to him. Promptly, effortlessly, he threw political economy away.

> It is said ... that the Bill offends against the principles of political economy. In one sense there is no doubt it is so. Political economy ... teaches you the best way of accumulating the most wealth in the shortest time ... But ... the object of the Bill was to give security to life; to save society from rushing down towards destruction; to give to property the security it is fast losing; to give confidence to people who will not trust each other; to break down the mischiefs and the abuses of centuries; and give some sort of common ground upon which people might unite ... it is by its likelihood of attaining these objects, and not by its conformity to the principles of political economy, that the Bill must be tried. The principles of political economy! Why, we violate them every day.[39]

IV

The passing of the 1870 Land Act was not the end of Lowe's involvement with the subject. It was the Treasury's job to deal with loan applications from tenants who wanted to buy their land. Lowe and his permanent secretary, Ralph Lingen, proceeded energetically to weed out tenants whose leases they thought were too long for them to need to buy, tenants who did not live exclusively from farming, and tenants proposing to re-let any part of the land once they had bought it. The result of such exertions, continued by Lowe's Conservative successor, was the loan of a modest £358,000 over the first seven years of the Act. Less than half of this went for purchases of less than 100 acres, where the price per acre was in any case much higher than for the large holdings.[40]

Lowe thus stood little chance that the Irish would admit him to their canon of benefactors. A speech late in 1871 defended his government's record in 'recalling of years of wrong and returning it at last to a policy of equity and justice', only for Lowe to reveal that, once again, he was talking about the disestablishment of the Church. A discreet veil of silence covered land reform.[41] In 1872 and again in 1873, Lowe opposed a motion to raise the pay scale for Irish civil servants to parity with England, telling them that their cost of living was lower, their duties were lighter, and that any Irishman who disliked his salary could apply for a job in Whitehall.[42] More damaging were Lowe's remarks, extraordinary even by his standards, when accepting the freedom of Glasgow in 1872. After a string of quips about his refusal as Chancellor to help the distressed Irish fishing industry, he went on to tell an anecdote about drunken Irish politicians rushing through the wrong door and falling fully clothed into a swimming-bath. Assorted Irish newspapers called him a 'cad' and a 'coward'.[43]

Cowardice is not the obvious charge against such a performance in Glasgow, and Lowe's remarks reinforce how lucky it was for everyone, except perhaps the Fenians, that Lowe had spent the years of the famine hidden away in Australia. What he was saying there about the squatters he would have translated, with minimal change, to fit the Irish peasantry. Indeed this is exactly what he later did. Both societies, in his view, were being held down in agrarian backwardness by a conservative class. That one was a rich minority and the other a poor majority made no difference to Lowe. Nor, in the light of his underlying principles, should it have.

7
Democratic Economics or Gladstonian Finance?

Lowe's attitude to democracy, like his attitude to everything else, was utilitarian, utility in its turn requiring that no class interest dominated the others. Who should get the vote, therefore, depended on the balance of social forces as well as the level of education. In Australia, this led him to a highly provisional endorsement of general male suffrage:

> Popular election is a great evil and is only to be endured because it is designed to work out a greater good. If we find the good does not exceed the evil, let us discard the principle altogether.[1]

Britain was another matter. The young Lowe, unlike the young Gladstone, had been a fervent supporter of the 1832 Reform Bill. (A speech in its favour at the Oxford Union had prompted a spectator, seeing from a distance only Lowe's mop of white hair, to ask who was the 'dear old gentleman' who had achieved such eloquence, though the eloquence won Lowe only four votes.) Lowe was always ready to expatiate on the glories of representative government, even discounting the value of ancient history because it studied societies which lacked it.[2] The question was how many people should be brought within the representative pale. Characteristically, Lowe saw even this question as a matter for individual effort as much as constitutional decision: 'If persons who live in £8 houses would only forego 120 quarts [of beer] annually, they might at once occupy a £10 house, and acquire the franchise.'[3]

This is from one of Lowe's speeches between 1865 and 1867 opposing the extension of the suffrage by act of parliament. It was these speeches, rated by the *Pall Mall Gazette* as among 'the most magnificent intellectual efforts ever witnessed within the walls of Parliament', which brought Lowe his greatest renown. The obituarists and Lowe's official biographer agreed that this, and not Lowe's Chancellorship, was the supreme moment in his life. Bryce, who thought him 'the equal in oratory and the superior in intellect' to Gladstone and Bright, recollected a

> political philosophy put in so terse and bright and pointed a form that it made the ordinary country gentleman fancy himself a philosopher... The bulk of the wealthier commercial class and a large section of the landed class... were then already beginning to pass through what was called Whiggism into habits of thought that were practically Tory. They did not know how far they had gone until Lowe's speeches told them.[4]

Two social levels up, Lord Lansdowne said Lowe's first anti-Reform speech had soothed his gout.[5]

In his speeches Lowe warned that the poor might be worse off under a wider franchise. More voters meant more expense in fighting a constituency, and the likely result was that most MPs would be 'millionaires to whom any expense is of no moment, [or] demagogues, who compensate for want of money by pandering to popular passions'.[6] Lowe contrasted this degenerate semi-plutocracy with the House since 1832, which had discharged its 'principal' function of finance 'with greater success than any other deliberative assembly'. And: 'can anyone say that the interests of the poor are neglected here?'[7]

This was far from a bestowal of perfection on the status quo. The legislature now had so much power that it was threatening the ministerial discretion on which competent government must rely. All the more reason not to extend the franchise, was Lowe's conclusion. The Founding Fathers of the USA had instituted separation of powers precisely because they intended a wide franchise from the start, and understood the consequences for the executive in a way apparently beyond the comprehension of the reform faction in Britain.

It was a spur, not a frustration, to Lowe that reform was coming in just as the building blocks were in place for a liberal society which, given a fair wind for a few years, would be able to survive democracy. Some of this conviction was based on his view, seen in Chapter 3, that the results of economic liberalisation would eventually convert people who had barely heard of Smith or Ricardo to a mentality which fitted their ideas. So indeed would many financial, industrial and social changes *not* obviously grounded in liberal legislation. Lowe, in Winter's (1976) words, was convinced that 'the factories, the railways, the telegraph, the advance of science, the awakened intelligence of the previously inert masses were rapidly making snobbery, deference, traditionalism and sentimentality obsolete and irrelevant'.[8] A new lease of life for these evils was not the obvious consequence of widening the franchise – though who knew what the 'plutocrat' MPs might bring in their wake? – but Lowe thought socialism and indeed Manchester dogmatism (a category from which he excluded himself) would also be casualties of progress if only the poorer classes could be denied political access to them for a few more years.

Meanwhile the Reformers did not even treat the poor logically. Instead of a sensible paternalism which would keep the franchise out of uneducated hands, many reformers seemed to want to enfranchise large sections of the working class so that they could elevate their own condition by compulsion.

> It were ludicrous, if it were not so sad, to hear speeches which urge working men to seek for the franchise, that they may compel Parliament to compel them to educate their children, or to practise an involuntary abstinence from intoxicating liquors.[9]

But Lowe's greatest fear was of the political economy the workers' representatives would bring into parliament with them. His warnings began in *The Times*, after Palmerston returned to power in 1859 with a lowering of the franchise in mind. Lowe invoked the steep taxes the richer classes could expect to pay if the franchise were doubled, to admit a large class of people who had amply demonstrated their ignorance of economics.

> The public burdens will be imposed by those who do not pay them... Our laws are now framed in accordance with the principles

> of political economy; but will they be likely to rest on that basis long when the legislative power has virtually passed into the hands of persons who believe they can raise the price of labour by diminishing its efficiency, and who consider that the shortest road to wealth is the destruction of that capital on which they must rely for subsistence?[10]

Lowe returned to the same theme in 1865, greeting with well-orchestrated disbelief Mill's claims that working-class electors would be too disunited to pursue their class interests through parliament, and would in any case be on the side of vigilance in keeping public spending down. Lowe scoffed at the first claim, though his own prediction of a lottery between millionaires and demagogues to sit for poorer areas rather went to uphold it. The second claim was one which would also be made by Gladstone. It was a plausible forecast, given the continuing appetite for retrenchment among working-class radicals who at this stage still saw the State as an instrument of oppression and exploitation. It was not, however, plausible to Lowe. History, he said, showed only one machinery that could be relied upon for public economy, and that was 'a popular Assembly representing the nation that provides the taxes'. Look at the improvement in the public finances since 1832, Lowe exclaimed. Compare them with France, where government spending was starting to come down at last, but on the whim of Louis Napoleon, a whim which might be reversed tomorrow. Neither princes nor workmen could be trusted to restrain public profligacy: 'the only real safeguard [is] the right of refusal' (to pay taxes).[11]

In his Commons speeches on the Second Reform Bill, Lowe broadened his attack. Not only would a majority working-class electorate lack incentive to curb spending charged up to others; its ignorance and refusal to take responsibility for its own conditions would ensure a massive extension of the State.

> The theory of uneducated and half-educated persons in general is, that Government is almost omnipotent, and that when an evil is not remedied the fault lies in the indolence, the selfishness, or the short-sightedness of Parliament.[12]

Such views would inevitably dominate, Lowe claimed, once power slipped 'from the hands of property and intelligence' to men 'whose whole life is necessarily occupied in daily struggles for existence'. It was *because* he was a Liberal, Lowe told the House, that he knew that 'by pure and clear intelligence alone can the cause of true progress be promoted'.[13] Nowhere was this more true than in the field of political economy:

> Protection, for instance, is the political economy of the poor, simply because they are not able to follow the chain of reasoning which demonstrates that they themselves are sure to be the victims of the waste of capital which protection implies.[14]

And anyone who wanted to see how democracy extinguished free trade need only look at Canada, New South Wales, Victoria and above all the USA.[15]

In 1867 the Conservative government succeeded in enacting a reform which gave the vote to far more men than the Liberals had first proposed. Initially the warnings of the Cassandra of Calne, as Lowe became known, seemed unfounded. In the first place, no reversal of free trade followed; as Howe (1997) observes: 'Almost uniquely, and against the expectation of many, in Britain the advent of democracy consolidated rather than undermined free trade.'[16] Not only did free trade survive, but working-class movements, far from demanding higher public spending, gave Gladstone reasonably friendly criticism for not being Gladstonian enough. 'Most radicals', in Biagini's (1991) words, still 'tended to consider the state an appendage of the upper classes and shared Adam Smith's view that it was inherently oppressive, incompetent, inefficient and corrupt'.[17] (The fact that 70 per cent of government expenditure was either military or devoted to servicing wartime debts did not help.) But, with a majority Conservative government installed after 1874, Lowe was swift to blame the climbing public expenditure of the 1870s on the new class of fully enfranchised, but only half-heartedly taxed, workers. As Disraeli's budgeting breached the £80 million mark, Lowe linked this with a resurgent Tory imperialism which fed effortlessly on 'the art by which one set of persons may be forced to pay for that which another set of persons have contrived to enjoy'.[18] And, as momentum built up in the late 1870s for yet another extension of the franchise, Lowe returned to the link between democracy and economic incompetence, even arguing that, if democracy there must be, it was best for it not even to try to understand political economy (see Chapter 3).

Within weeks of this Lowe found a rich new (or renewed) target in the form of 'Mr Gladstone on Manhood Suffrage'. Gladstone's article in the *Fortnightly Review* had denied that the poor, once enfranchised, would instantly use this power to strip the rich of their wealth, and bring economy and society down. The rich might be more competent at governing, but the poor were far more unselfish and disinterested. Lowe had said as much himself in 1865, warning that democracy would involve the nation in many a 'just' war.[19] Now he accused Gladstone of proclaiming 'the love of the poorer classes for inequality . . . We are invited to give them equality because they hate it'. If this were true, said Lowe, it would be the best reason yet for not giving them the vote. Yes, inequality was inevitable, but to make an 'idol' of it you would need a mind of such 'meanness and perverseness' as to disqualify its owner from any political say. Anyway, the poor did not love inequality. They might be dazzled by pomp and grateful for kind treatment by superiors, but none of this would stop them falling victim to unscrupulous leaders. And, Lowe wrapped up the argument triumphantly, if they loved inequality, could Mr Gladstone explain why they were mostly on the parliamentary side in the Civil War?[20]

II

Gladstone had had 20 years to get used to Lowe rebutting things he had not said, and Lowe taking him to task for his democratic tendencies. Gladstone's budget speech of 1860 had raised several alarms in Lowe, most of all when Gladstone conflated the state of the national finances with the state of the government's intentions to widen the franchise. Mr Gladstone, said Lowe, had 'called on the present Parliament to create the deficit, but reserved to their successors the task of filling up the void'. Nor had Gladstone left any doubt what kind of successors he had in mind, 'the representatives of the hitherto unenfranchised masses' whom, most ominously, Gladstone clearly believed 'had wrongs to avenge as well as duties to discharge'.[21]

> Who does not see in this preliminary steps to that state of things against which we have so long felt it our duty to protest, when the

> duties of the poor and rich will be finally divided from each other – the duty of the poor being to impose, and that of the rich to pay the taxes.[22]

Already Gladstone was taking off indirect taxes and even hinting at graduated income tax to come in the next year.

The hint led nowhere, but Lowe's anxieties were revived in 1863 when Gladstone announced that he had no objection in principle to progressive taxation but did wonder whether it was either 'practicable' or 'safe'.

> The vice of the principle in which Mr Gladstone can see nothing wrong is simply its injustice. It is the treating of wealth as a crime, and poverty as a merit. The State should, above all things, be no respecter of persons. The Queen herself submits to pay the Income Tax.[23]

And what was safety in this context, inquired Lowe, if it was not a matter of principle? No departure from proportional taxation was safe because once you left that firm and rigid path, you stepped straight into a swamp of arbitrariness, prejudice and class conflict. You could not go beyond proportional taxation 'without shaking the very basis of that property on which modern society reposes. Figures are deaf, impassive and impartial, but if we go beyond figures what rest shall we find for the sole of our foot?' You might end up with progressive taxation like the US, or regressive taxation like ancien regime France. Either way you would have removed the only 'common principle on which the burdens of state can be adjusted', and could look forward to one part of the community 'under the plausible pretext of equity and humanity, [plundering] another class'. The only uncertainty was who would be the plunderer and who the plundered.[24]

A speech of Gladstone's in October 1864 raised a different spectre in Lowe's mind. An address to Gladstone had been presented by Charles Robertson, president of the Liverpool Financial Reform Association, in which he expressed the hope that indirect taxes would eventually be abolished, called for the immediate end to duties on tea, sugar and coffee, and reassured Gladstone how little he would have to put on income tax in their place. Gladstone's response was that 'Direct taxation, I admit if we were to proceed on abstract principles, is a sound principle; but, gentlemen, have some compassion upon those whose first necessity, whose first duty it is to provide for the maintenance of the public credit.'[25]

To Lowe the message was clear: the Chancellor now had in his sights a utopia where direct taxation alone supported the State. Some members of Gladstone's audience had alleged that 'true' free trade excluded indirect taxation, and Gladstone, instead of condemning this reduction of a 'noble and true' theory to absurdity, had chosen instead to muse on the purely political difficulties of getting rid of indirect taxes.[26] Yet again, Lowe admonished, Gladstone was toying with a proposal which would have one class imposing all the burdens on another class, and so divide the nation into two hostile camps.[27]

Taken overall, Lowe's leaders in *The Times* gave Gladstone's second Chancellorship (1859–66) considerably less than half marks. The style, to Lowe, was if anything worse than the content – indeed it dictated many of the faults in the content.

Lowe had already, in an article of 1857, marked Gladstone down as 'a casuist in a pragmatic age, luxuriating in the metaphysics of finance... [His] additions are performed in a species of oratorical ecstasy, and his subtractions are made with the violence of a paroxysm'.[28] Now, with Gladstone back as Chancellor, the paroxysms continued – Gladstone's superabundant energy made them inescapable, Lowe explained[29] – but the atmosphere of devotional solemnity had given way to a sharp operator with a nice line in fly-by-night short-termism. (At times Lowe manages to sound like a rather conventional Tory backbencher 'savaging' Harold Wilson at a constituency fete some time in the 1960s.) Had Gladstone given any thought, Lowe inquired in 1860, to how he was going to maintain the hasty expedients temporarily financing the cost of the French treaty?[30] What would happen in the event of a major war? Would the Treasury emerge as peacemaker simply by running out of money to pay for it? There *were* two minor wars on hand, but fortunately both were so remote 'that we cannot bring ourselves to feel a very thrilling interest in the results... We have the double satisfaction of being at rest ourselves and contemplating the troubles and turmoils of others.'

With one inevitable exception:

> As well expect the caged tiger to cease pacing backwards and forwards within his narrow limits as suppose that any vacation, any time of relaxation or quiet, can lull to rest the morbid activity of our Chancellor of the Exchequer... He is always managing for us some charming little surprise... He is a perfect master of the suddenly disagreeable. He has effectually divorced the idea of surprise from the idea of pleasure... he has, indeed, considerable claims, in this quiet and steady-going country, to take rank as the inventor of a new science, which may, perhaps, be known to future ages under the name of financial thamaturgy.[31]

This seems to have been provoked by Gladstone's intent to collect income tax quarterly instead of twice a year. And, after the budget of 1861, Lowe again berated the Chancellor's unsettled and unsettling behaviour.

> We object to a Chancellor of the Exchequer who is always at war with the revenue. We don't want to be involved in apparently inextricable difficulty in order that we may be saved by some financial miracle... we protest against being laden with artificial anxieties, and not the less because so long as a budget is such a tour de force there is only one man in England who would wish to have the task of proposing it.[32]

But the tone changed abruptly in 'Mr Gladstone's Financial Statements', which Lowe published in the *Home and Foreign Review* in 1864: 'a valuable study', says Professor Winter, 'for anyone who wants to experience the full force of the mid-Victorian liberal passion for retrenchment'.[33] Now Gladstone was the man who had heroically saved income tax, that hated but necessary imposition which had been due to lapse when he first assumed office in 1853. Alone he was keeping public spending down, now that parliament had thrown over its role as economiser and was egging on the government to find new ways of spending money: Lowe dreaded what would happen when Gladstone went.[34] Above all Gladstone, in Professor Winter's paraphrase of Lowe, 'had accomplished one of the great quiet revolutions of the modern age – he had found economy and society restricted, protectionist and monopolistic and had made it free, expanding and open to enterprise'.[35]

When, in December 1868, Lord Acton asked Gladstone why he had chosen Lowe as his Chancellor, Gladstone cited this article. And, while he had no doubt enjoyed the praise of himself, it was most likely Lowe's list of gaps in the Gladstonian achievement to date that convinced Gladstone that here was the right man to carry on the good work – work not just incomplete but in peril from the new-found 'generosity' of parliament. How far the Reform Bill had increased this peril was something on which they could, for the moment, agree to disagree.

8
Saying No

'I wish they would make me Chancellor of the Exchequer', Lowe had confided to Lady Salisbury in September 1868, in a broadside against the profligacy of Disraeli's first government. 'I think I possess the faculty of saying No as well as anyone and in that and not in superfine finance lies the real secret of financial prosperity.'[1] Now, three months later, he *was* Chancellor, appointed by a prime minister to whom saying No was ever a major virtue, albeit one which sprung from roots little recognised by Lowe. In Professor Winter's words, Gladstone 'was a passionate economiser because he had a social conscience; Lowe was a zealous economiser because he was a rationalist.'[2] On 26 December 1868 Gladstone sent Lowe a long memorandum 'trust[ing] to your indulgence in volunteering any suggestion', and restating his confidence that Lowe could hold public spending down. The job was the hardest in the cabinet, Gladstone warned, not least because Lowe would find that whenever he *did* recommend any new expenditure, all those ministers whose demands he had refused 'will look out with a preterhuman sharpness for the joints in your own armour'. If the proposals then failed to get through parliament, Lowe could expect to feel like 'an ancient soldier wounded in the back'. But, said Gladstone, he must not start moralising at Lowe and 'was it not too late, I would tell you here that you may skip the last two pages'.[3]

Lowe had just been to his constituency of London university to tell them he intended no kindnesses towards 'that most susceptible part of an Englishman's person, the pocket of his trousers'.[4] At a Liberal banquet in Gloucester to celebrate the election victory he declaimed that 'all highly-refined and complicated financial operations avail very little, and there is only one secret to insure prosperity and that is to spend much less than you receive'.[5] Now he started work at a Treasury which was already busy stiffening the sinews of frugality. In 1861 Gladstone, as Chancellor, had established the principle that the Treasury should scrutinise all other departments' estimates in detail before they went before parliament. The next year he established the Commons' Public Accounts Committee. In 1863 Gladstone put the practice of switching unspent revenue to some other project (virement) under severe restraint in the hope that such money would now come back to him. The Comptroller and Auditor General, a post created in the 1866 Exchequer and Audit Act, could refuse authorisation of spending by any other department, and was also charged with examining departmental books, to make sure they were spending their money as intended when parliament granted it. In 1868, shortly before Lowe became Chancellor, departments had additionally been compelled to get Treasury permission before they increased civil servants' salaries or pensions.[6]

But as Chancellor, Lowe was to discover how many gaps this left in his powers of economy. The Treasury was normally excluded from the actual planning of policy, and hence expenditure, by other departments. To say no to the sum of money which emerged at the end of the process, quite possibly forcing a resentful colleague to tear up his plans and do the work over again, was a power which even Lowe could not use on every occasion he would have liked.[7] Defence spending, where the departments concerned could usually shake the Treasury off simply by deploying their superior technical knowledge, was a problem in its own right.

But, where he could, Lowe used his powers to the full. 'The first thing I did as Chancellor of the Exchequer', he said at the end of his term, 'was to issue an order to the Treasury that no new expenditure whatever be allowed without my opinion first being taken on it'.[8] There was to be no burying his head in high finance while some lowly official tried to hold back the demands of permanent secretaries and cabinet ministers. Exactly how trivial a request needed to be to avoid Lowe's gaze is unclear from the Treasury records, but it *is* clear that its surveillance took on a microscopic quality once Lowe was installed at No. 11. Every schoolboy knows the Victorian Treasury existed to refuse an increased pension to the periodic admiral's widow; but the sums involved here were huge compared with the proposed pay rise for the doorkeeper at the Post Office at Alexandria, or the £3 3s. 2d. for new coconut matting and repairs to the stove at Thame County Court in Oxfordshire.[9]

And Lowe was ever ready to press some very detailed economies onto colleagues. Some greatly resented the interference. Thus, when Lowe asked Lord Clarendon, the Foreign Secretary, why he needed to have an Anglican chaplain in every Chinese port, Clarendon asked Gladstone to remind Lowe 'that because he holds the purse strings, he is not to pull all the other strings'.[10]

'Chaplains for China' never reached the public domain, but some of Lowe's other economies were of extremely high profile. During the Franco-Prussian war of 1870 he refused to pay for the repatriation of British citizens stranded in Paris and unable to pay for themselves. Contrary to those who saw this as an act of humanity so exceptional as to set no precedent, Lowe warned that it 'will entirely alter the principles on which the Treasury acts in these cases which are of very frequent occurrence'.[11] Three months later he was urging Gladstone to reduce the salary of one of their cabinet colleagues. Not only did the Irish Secretary live in a house 'ridiculously large for the office', but his policy of 'pacifying Ireland by giving dinners at the public expense' was contemptible and 'has met with just the success which it deserved'.[12] A new Attorney- and Solicitor-General in November 1871 were, to Lowe, a good opportunity for reducing these two salaries as well. We should pay no more than is needed to get adequate candidates, Lowe told Gladstone: the new law officers were, after all, rich enough to have got into parliament in the first place, surely proof that the simple honour of becoming law officers would now be enough for them, and little money need be offered.

Lowe then refused to buy Epping Forest for the nation on the grounds that Londoners would be the main users and London should therefore pay for it. A speech in Glasgow in 1872 distilled these episodes into a treatise and self-assessment in the art of refusal.

> Some people are said to have the art which one great man is reported to have had, who when people came to ask favours of him, 'kicked them downstairs with so charming a grace that he seemed to be handing them up.' Unhappily, that talent has been

> entirely denied to me. I say nothing about the former part, but the latter is totally lacking.[13]

On this last point opinions differed. When the Licensed Victuallers' Association visited Lowe, its chairman reported that 'the great scholar and debater cheered the meeting with many sunny glimpses of his own anti-puritan character'. *The Times* in its turn congratulated the chairman on his 'poetic' account of the meeting.[14] But Lowe was now Home Secretary and no money was involved. His dominant style was set early in his career, when, to a deputation of Australian bankers who claimed they 'could not live' if a certain proposal went through, he snapped 'And pray, why should you live?'[15]

Lowe's most celebrated No – certainly the one which did most to confirm the popular view of him – was his refusal in 1872 to contribute towards an expedition to look for the missing Dr Livingstone in Africa (despite the Treasury's earlier burst of generosity in giving Livingstone £10 to buy presents for African chiefs).[16] This came in useful the following year when he used it as a precedent for refusing any public money for an archaeological dig at the site of Troy.

> Shall it be said that a large number of wealthy English noblemen and gentlemen can find no better expedient of a liberal curiosity than to ask the Chancellor of the Exchequer to employ, for its satisfaction, money wrung from the earnings of the poorest of the community? I sincerely regret that the spirit of Herodes Atticus has not descended to modern times, and feel convinced that if half of the energy which is devoted in attempts to obtain aid from the Government were given to create a spirit of private munificence, this and many similar objects might be attained with the utmost facility and completeness.[17]

Science fared little better. Refusing money to the Scottish Meteorological Society, Lowe was made to listen to a list of all the scientific bodies which did enjoy government support. Lowe replied that he would have to do something about this, and sent the meteorologists on their way with the thought that 'Nothing impairs or relaxes the efforts of voluntary societies more than the receiving of government money, and I really believe that if I were to give you £300, I should be doing you the greatest unkindness of which I could possibly be guilty.'[18]

Softening Lowe's public persona at the Treasury was Acton Smee Ayrton, the commissioner of Works. Lowe was lucky to have this appalling pasteboard caricature of himself installed in a ministry whose spending decisions were as high profile as his own. Both Ayrton's ferocious parsimony and his vivid insolence to all comers contrived to make Lowe look judicious and moderate by comparison. When Ayrton insisted on a cramped but cheap site for the new Law Courts (the one they occupy today), Lowe tried to get the plans changed to a more spacious location on the Embankment. In this he failed, but drew level with Ayrton over the arguably less important issue of whether sewage from Windsor Castle should mix with that of common people. When the Queen's consternation at the prospect was communicated to Lowe, he overruled Ayrton and provided for a special island in the Thames to process the royal waste, commenting that 'I have achieved the drainage of Windsor and I die happy.'[19]

One of Lowe's odder responsibilities as Chancellor was to defend the Attorney-General's decisions to prosecute or not to prosecute, on the grounds that public money was involved. When the claimant to the Tichborne estate was arraigned for fraud, his noisy band of parliamentary supporters naturally desired to know why their man was being prosecuted while the government had stayed out of the Overend Gurney banking scandal as being a 'private matter'. Rather than merely defending the decision, Lowe happily told parliament that he expected the claimant to be found guilty, given a civil jury's obvious disbelief in his story. No one, not even the claimant's party, seemed to think there was anything wrong with the Chancellor of the Exchequer's intervention in a pending court case.[20]

But Lowe was soon to change his mind about the cost of the prosecution. When he belatedly discovered that the Attorney-General was sending barristers to Australia and Chile, each furnished with a blank cheque to bring home any witness who might be of any use, he sent Gladstone a frantic telegram asking him to intercept the arrangement. Gladstone was not pleased when the wire arrived at Hawarden in the middle of the night, but nonetheless agreed with Lowe, albeit on the slightly different grounds that unlimited spending by one of the sides in the trial would vitiate 'a prevailing steady popular belief' in its fairness.[21]

II

Although Lowe had been put at the Treasury because he was an economiser, some of his economising spirit stemmed for his move to the Treasury. His handling of the South Kensington Museum is a good example. As vice president of the Board of Education, he had supported the museum's efforts to get more money from the government. Sir Henry Cole, now the Museum's director after 30 years of public service that had included pioneering the penny post with Rowland Hill, bringing together the cast which put on the Great Exhibition, and inventing the Christmas card, was even egged on by Lowe to be more demanding on the public purse. Lowe's about turn as Chancellor came as a severe shock to Cole, still the museum's director, particularly when Lowe's economising began to incorporate demands for 'relevance', the Chancellor objecting to the purchase of a collection of armour 'because it had no use at the present day' – a strange way to choose exhibits for a museum.[22]

Lowe had no monopolistic designs on cheeseparing ideas, and hoped to receive suggestions from outside the Treasury. He hoped in vain. From those outside parliament, he complained, he could look only to requests for new taxes. A Liberal audience in Gloucester laughed as Lowe berated careless people who burned their fingers on matches, ugly people who found that the camera did not lie, and sleepless people enduring the neighbour's piano practice – one and all types who would write to the Chancellor demanding a duty on the offending article.[23] Parliament itself was no better. It was, Lowe said at the end of his Chancellorship, divided into economisers and spenders. But somehow they were never present at the same time, one party finding its voice when generalities were the agenda, the other arriving in time to debate specifics; the reason being that 'everybody is in favour of economy in the abstract and most people are in favour of extravagance in the concrete.'[24]

And Lowe had little patience with vague calls for retrenchment which gave no hint of what was to be retrenched. When, in 1872, Vernon Harcourt MP proposed a resolution about 'excessive public spending', Lowe told him it was no use talking about public spending in the abstract. Economy could only be achieved 'by inquiring into minute matters of detail, and by repulsive labour from which men naturally shrink.'[25] Nor was it any use fixing a ceiling for taxation and cutting public spending back accordingly: the House must decide what public spending was necessary, the Chancellor then had to find taxation to cover it and 'for my part I heartily wish that the House of Commons would put pressure and duress on me for the purpose of making me more economical than I am.'[26] In particular, Lowe invited the House to censure the government if it 'be going into what is called a spirited foreign policy, if it is going to intermeddle with the affairs of our neighbours, if we seek to play a leading part in the affairs of Europe which are not our immediate concern'. But in fact the government meant to do none of these things. If they had raised defence spending, that was because they had found the Army in 'a state disgraceful to the nation'. (Lowe was talking about the purchase of commissions, and the high public cost of ending the practice.)[27] MPs should also remember that there were five million more people to govern than in 1851 'and we have undertaken to educate them' – a reference to Forster's 1870 Education Act. Where the government *had* saved public money was in its refusal to do things which private individuals could do just as well without the government. Giving into this would mean not just higher taxes, but

> We chill the very foundations of charity and encourage people, instead of doing the best they can with their money, to look to the Government for help. Nothing is more true than the opinion expressed by an hon. Member of this House that a paternal government means a childish people. We are occasionally taunted with not being paternal; but of all the disgraceful epithets which can be bestowed upon a government I think that is about the worst.[28]

And if setting the government's face against paternalism made it unpopular on occasion, putting up taxes made it unpopular on every occasion. Chancellors must accept that their popularity will track the business cycle and that, if they are to achieve a reasonable lifespan, it will not be given to them to dwell only in good times:

> I can imagine few positions more agreeable than that of the Chancellor of the Exchequer in prosperous times, particularly when he has the good fortune to be surrounded by very economical colleagues. They rise early, they sit up late, and know no rest, in

> order to save money for the public, and the Chancellor of the Exchequer, who has had only a very small share in their labour, comes down once a year like a benignant fairy to scatter blessings o'er the land, for which he frequently gets very undeserved credit and applause.[29]

This being so, justice was done overall if he gets 'perhaps undeserved censure' in hard times.[30]

No doubt Lowe's cabinet colleagues enjoyed his gentle sarcasm about their devotion to parsimony. Lowe himself was much less amused in 1873 when some of them swung behind another 'economy' motion by Vernon Harcourt, to back his 'proposed Committee on Miscellaneous Civil Expenditure'. On 15 February 1873 Lowe wrote to Gladstone:

> I think it rather hard after having taken an amount of labour on myself which no Chancellor of the Exchequer ever took before in keeping down the Expenditure of the Civil Service Estimates and having succeeded beyond my expectations I should be [illegible] by the head of the Government as just the person whose work in his opinion most needs the revision of a Parliamentary Committee.[31]

Worse was to follow. While Lowe thought any such committee an affront to the Treasury, at least its original terms of reference had been specifically to enquire into civil expenditure not 'under the direct or effectual control of the Treasury'. Now it turned out that

> The attack is . . . to be made against the treatment of the Writers . . . a class of persons whose . . . management is in the hands of the Treasury . . . Further this has been done as we are told by Childers in order to prove that the Treasury has been guilty of gross extravagance . . . Further this step has been taken and matters put I fear beyond recall without giving me the least intimation.[32]

Gladstone did not reply. He just wrote at the end 'Surely exaggerated'. With Lowe as his Chancellor, he might as well have had the words mounted on a rubber stamp.

9
The Chancellor Meets His Match

Lowe inherited a fiscal State which, in the Tories' last full year in office, had spent £71,236,000, around 9 per cent of national income. Of this, £2 million was a special grant to finance the Abyssinian expedition. Of the remainder, three-eighths was devoted to servicing the debt, and three-eighths to ordinary military (including Indian military) expenditure. The cost of tax collection accounted for 4 per cent of spending, and the (profitable) outlay on posts and telegraphs 5 per cent. That left £10,385,000 for expenditure on civil administration, of which two-thirds came under three headings: law and justice (£3,021,000), civil service and diplomatic salaries and expenses (£2,276,100) and education (£1,597,400). Most of the rest comprised public works and buildings and the upkeep of the monarchy.

Of the revenue of £69,600,000, nearly two-thirds came from customs (£22,650,000) or excise (£20,162,000). Income tax (raised from 4d. to 5d. in the £ halfway through the Tories' last fiscal year) yielded £6,840,000, stamp duty £9,541,000 and 'assessed taxes' (mainly land and house taxes) £3,109,000. Nearly £6.5 million was earned by the government, three-fifths of it from the post office, but with £1.7 million coming in from services rendered by the armed forces, half of this from India.

On the subject of taxation, Lowe had set out his position early on. In an 1857 editorial he anticipated the modern Laffer curve, arguing that low rates of tax brought in more revenue than high ones.

> We have found the philosopher's stone . . . in the simple readjustment of the principles of taxation according to laws suggested by

> nature and reaffirmed by science as embodying truth at once of abstract simplicity and purity and perfectly practical application... these things have been to us a fountain of abundance, an inexhaustible cornucopia, a talisman of ever-renewed wealth and power... To raise a large revenue with less trouble than we formerly did with a small one, combining an increase of our income with a lightening of our burdens is a feat so extraordinary that we have a right to accuse of wilful obliquity those who will not follow in a direction which theory and practice alike unite to recommend.[1]

It was just as important that no single tax should press too heavily. By 1857 Gladstone was attacking the Chancellor of the day, Sir George Cornewall Lewis, for preserving an overcomplex and expensive fiscal machinery in the name of equal treatment for all. Gladstone called for fewer and simpler taxes and showed no excessive grief that some interests would thus receive heavier burdens than others. His aim, he said, was 'to simplify our fiscal system by concentrating its pressure on a few well chosen articles of extended consumption'.[2] Lowe from the start sided with Lewis.[3] Initially he directed his remarks to India, encouraging the Chancellor to remember that taxes on income, houses, death, property, equipages, carriages, horses and elephants were only 'samples of the powerful instruments which hang on the walls of the armoury of the Chancellor of the Exchequer'.[4]

The contrast between Gladstone and Lewis was picked out by Baysinger and Tollison (1980). In an ingenious article they located Gladstone as a precursor of the modern Virginia School of public choice theory. According to James Buchanan, the school's leader, neoclassical balancing acts in the style of Cornewall Lewis, searching for a Pareto-efficient distribution of the tax burden and inevitably recommending an egalitarian lightness of touch across the fiscal keyboard, miss the point by taking the size of the government's budget as exogenous. And this leads to precisely the kind of fiscal system least able to keep appetites for public spending in check. The fewer the taxes, the lower the overall rate of tax that politicians will dare impose. 'Pressing lightly' is a vice, not a virtue, in Virginian eyes.

In fact Gladstone makes a doubtful Virginian. He certainly said more than once that abolishing income tax, if it could be achieved, would 'tend to public economy'.[5] But whether it could be achieved itself depended on prior retrenchment. And this reflected Gladstone's general order of priorities. The amount of necessary expenditure must first be ascertained and then taxes found to finance it. As long ago as 1848, Gladstone had complained to his brother that Cobden first made up his mind which taxes should and should not be suffered, and then insisted that spending be cut to fit the resulting revenue. This, said Gladstone, was the opposite of responsible government.[6]

But if the 'Virginian' label sits awkwardly on Gladstone, the 'neo-classical' cap fits Lowe to perfection. Becoming Chancellor himself only stretched his appetite for egalitarian complexity in the tax system. Previous Chancellors, he said a few months after taking office, had been inclined to put too many eggs into too few baskets. That was one reason why he was standing here today defending the life of the house tax. (The other was that McCulloch and Mill had persuaded him that it was better geared to ability to pay than almost any other tax.)[7]

But if the array of taxes was to be complex, it mattered all the more to Lowe that each constituent tax be simple. This meant a minimum of exemptions. On the brink of his first budget, he had to deal with a motion from George Whalley, Liberal MP for Peterborough, that income tax be repealed 'on trade, profits and personal property of all kinds; and that any deficiency be raised by an increased tax on land and fixed property'. 'I believe, with Adam Smith', retorted Lowe, that all men should be taxed according to ability to pay. Anyone who disagreed should not be amending exemptions around the income tax. Logically they must abolish it altogether.

> The notion of income is one very difficult to seize. It is like 'now.' In a moment it flies from you when you stop. It is the notion of man's annual revenue abstracted altogether from the sources from whence it comes and the purposes for which it goes. That is the idea of an income; and the moment you begin to say you ought to pay more on this schedule and less on that, or abolish, as the hon. Gentleman says, a schedule altogether, you are not amending the income tax, but destroying it, and making, instead of it, an unfair and bungling property tax. Unless you look at income without reference to the sources, whence it comes or whither it goes, it is impossible to maintain an income tax by any argument.

> You cannot make any difference by looking at the destination of income; and whencesoever it comes, if it is raised under the protection of the Government, it ought to contribute to the Government.[8]

To say that everyone protected by the State should pay for that protection, irreproachable sentiment that it is, is of no help in deriving the doctrine that all incomes be taxed equally. The real basis of Lowe's argument is, once again, that once you start making exemptions, you put the question of who pays what into the arena of class politics, and no longer have an objective case for exempting any income from exemption.[9]

Lowe presented his first budget on 8 April 1869. *The Times* had just pronounced the financial situation more or less satisfactory, calculating indeed that if Lowe could restrain himself from tax cuts, he might have a surplus of £1.5 million over the forthcoming financial year.[10] Lowe's own forecast was less genial. The Abyssinian expedition of 1868 was now over, but the borrowing on its behalf still had to be paid back – a 'no change' budget would only just break even, and this only thanks to the 'heroic efforts' of the incoming war ministers to find economies in the Army and Navy.

Some of the Abyssinian borrowing had been necessitated by the outgoing Chancellor's miscalculations over the rest of the budget. Ward Hunt had ended up with twice the deficit he had planned for. Planning for deficits was not to be Lowe's style; deficits unplanned even less so.

And so Lowe faced the House in an apparently cautious and sombre mood on 8 April. As he produced the balance sheet for the year just gone and estimates for its successor, the first part of his speech skilfully deepened the gloom. 'Without any appearance of design', *The Times* commented the following day, 'in the most natural way in the world, the Chancellor led his hearers through a Lenten season of despair and then burst upon them in a sort of Easter festival of abundance'.[11]

Not a bad metaphor, but Easter is widely anticipated. Lowe's astounded colleagues heard that income tax would be cut by 1d. in the pound and the 1s. per quarter duty on corn consigned to a pre-enlightened age, swiftly joined by duties on fire insurance – 'a tax on prudence' – and hair powder (which had been bringing in all of

£925 a year). His happiness was especially palpable as he ended the residual 1s. per quarter corn duty that had survived 1846, an 'odious' tax that pressed most heavily on the poor, oppressed production at every stage and 'in every way' violated the principles of political economy.[12] Lowe made concessions towards the 'free breakfast table' enthusiasts and the cab trade by abolishing licence duties on the vendors of tea, coffee and cocoa, and the tax per mile, though not the standing licence, on cabs. And at the end of this £3 million handover he estimated a surplus of £438,000 for 1869–70.

How? The means, described by all except Lowe's predecessor as 'brilliant', was utterly simple. Until now, a quarter of the income tax for any financial year had been payable after the start of its successor on 6 April – thus for 1867–8 taxpayers had paid half their levy in October, a quarter in January and a quarter in mid-April. Lowe scooped the lot into January, so that 1869–70, uniquely, would collect five quarters' worth of tax. Sensitive perhaps to Adam Smith's four canons of taxation which included 'convenience of payment', Lowe suggested that under the old system 'to the poor it must be an immense vexation to be dunned in shillings and sixpences, while rich people would rather, I presume, pay the tax once and be done with it'.[13] From the Treasury's point of view, 1869 would borrow from 1870, 1870 from 1871 and so on. He did not know what would happen when the world came to an end, but in the meantime it was as if the nation had been presented with the money by the emperor of China.

Lowe did not stop at income tax. Land and assessed taxes in general were brought fully into the year in which they had been incurred. Thus Lowe derived extra revenue from the land tax, house tax, taxes on male servants, horses and armorial bearings.[14] And, he continued, some of the additional yield would be permanent. Too much revenue was currently being lost as taxpayers moved away, died or went bankrupt while the Inland Revenue stayed its hand; not to mention the evasion practised by those affecting to forget 'whether Dobbin had died on April 5th or 6th'.[15]

The budget's leading critic was Lowe's Conservative predecessor, Ward Hunt. Lowe's speech had extended an especial sympathy to Hunt for getting his forecasts wrong – any Chancellor estimating the succession duties might be hit by a shortage of deaths. Hunt agreed: 'the weather being exceedingly mild, wealthy testators contrived to live longer than usual, and Mr Lowe, with his usual luck, will have a crop of them this year'.[16] This time Hunt's estimate was dead right. But he also complained that, thanks to the budget, income tax payers would have to pay for five quarters in the current financial year. Lowe brushed this off with ease. So what? he retorted. If taxpayers had half their annual levy retarded by three months and only a quarter of it advanced by the same period, that made the new system less burdensome than the old, in 1869/70 or any other year.[17]

Oddly, Hunt ran his strictures on Lowe's invention alongside a claim on the patent for himself, pointing out that Lowe was only doing with income tax what he, Hunt, had already done with dog licences. Lowe might well have felt that if Hunt had had so radical an idea and then lacked the wit to bestow it on anything better than dogs, he was now getting his deserts.

But the financial community shared misgivings about the new way of collecting taxes, fearing that the lumpier the outgoings of the private sector, the harder for the Bank of England to sell bonds smoothly and keep interest rates steady. To this Lowe replied that this problem did not exist, that if it did exist he would relieve it by expedients 'not yet matured', and that the Bank's problems were none of his business.[18]

This was a classic case of three retorts being worse than one, but when January 1870 came round the Bank's fears did prove illusory. Its main concern, in any case, was over the monetary repercussions of the total amount of revenue the Chancellor took, not of its timing. In his 1870 budget speech Lowe conceded that the Bank had a case but not that he could do anything about it. If the revenue were unexpectedly large (as it now was, and would stay so while Lowe held office), money was scarce and dear, while if the government drew its balances down, 'you make the Bank poor and that will create a panic, and everyone knows that a panic is only another name for dear money'. With infuriating calm Lowe concluded that, since whatever he did, did mischief, 'I cannot either way escape my inexorable critic [and] had better go my own way; look after my affairs, and leave it to the moneyed interest to take care of theirs.'[19]

This was delivered against the background of the largest surplus any Chancellor had ever had at his disposal. The Army and Navy ministers had continued their 'heroic and patriotic exertions' to yield economies far beyond the first instalment Lowe had enjoyed the previous year. As for tax revenue, it was the highest on record in peacetime, exceeding Lowe's estimate in his previous budget by nearly £2 million. As Hunt had predicted, the rich people who had waited until they could die under a Liberal government were now doing so. As Lowe himself had predicted, the reforms to assessed taxes had radically reduced evasion: an effect he had, cautiously, omitted to estimate the previous year.

Lowe cut income tax by another penny, to 4d. in the pound. He halved the duty on sugar, and abolished the duties hitherto paid by papermakers, soap-makers, still-makers, watchmakers (provided the watch had less than two ounces of gold) and sellers of playing cards. The foothawker's licence was also abolished, Lowe commenting sympathetically that no one became a hawker in the first place unless they were in a bad way and had tried everything else. Critics feared the measure would encourage vagrancy.[20]

None of these taxes was bringing in serious revenue, and their abolition was no breach of Lowe's 'everyone must pay' doctrine, which he proceeded to reiterate in a metaphor which was to be quoted for a long time. Lowe invoked

> little animals at the bottom of the ocean under a pressure of three tons to the square inch. How do they contrive to live under such conditions? Because the pressure is equalised; and that should be the principle of taxation.[21]

If his opponents were to be consistent, Lowe went on, they should apply their principles to physical as well as fiscal pain, and 'pick out a certain number of persons, drive them raving mad with tic doloreux or gout, and exempt the rest of the community'. That, concluded Lowe with a touch of superfluity, 'is not just'. He himself was going to contrive to make everybody a little uneasy.[22]

If so he failed. The budget was as popular as its predecessor, though one of his measures made a few people decidedly uneasy. For the first time, Lowe imposed a new tax. On becoming Chancellor he had assured a Liberal audience that 'in the present highly developed and completely finished state of the science of taxation I should as little think of taking credit for a new tax as for inventing a new torture'.[23] But now he proposed a new tax: a licence of £1 per handgun – a response, he said, to an increasingly gun-loving society.

Improvements in firearms meant that 'we have undoubtedly obtained a considerable increase over the brute creation and in our power to exterminate savages. On the other hand, we buy these somewhat questionable advantages exceedingly dear' when the criminal or Irish terrorist could now hold 'six men's lives in their power'.[24]

Overall, Lowe had cut direct and indirect taxes by about the same amount. This was his usual goal, in line with his usual principle that tax burdens, and relief therefrom, be fairly split between rich and poor. On this occasion, however, he allowed himself some even more general remarks about the merits of direct and indirect taxes. He declined to follow Gladstone's 1861 flight of fancy in which the two forms of tax had become two sisters of equal but different attractions, to whom it was not just gallant but sensible for a Chancellor to pay equal court. Instead he dropped prosaically into the fact that in the end you could avoid indirect taxes by not buying the goods. (As a good libertarian he saw this as one of indirect taxation's charms.) They were, however, more costly to collect. Direct taxes had the drawback that 'you force a man to pay at a time when payment may be ruin' – a perilous argument from the man who had just ordered income tax to be levied in a single annual swoop.[25]

But more central to Lowe's argument this time was the perennial question of tax cuts versus debt reduction. He could have cut taxes by more, he told the House – after all, there was still an estimated surplus after everything he had done. But it would be reckless to do so. Peace might reign at the moment, but peace was easily broken.

> the indiscretion of a subordinate official – half a dozen glasses of wine too much, drunk by someone in a responsible situation – the merest accident may involve us in trouble from which there is no refuge except in enormous outlay.[26]

Lowe was justifying a restraint no one was asking him to break. Most critics wanted him to cut taxes by less and reduce the debt by more. Thus *The Times* accused Lowe of speaking strongly for debt reduction only to ignore his own good advice.[27]

But Lowe's actual remarks had been more even-handed than *The Times* was alleging. In fact his speech had carefully weighed the arguments on each side. Politically it made more sense to use a surplus to cut taxes, not in a cynical spirit to buy popularity, but to get people used to the idea of taxes, rather than the debt, varying with economic conditions. You could then say to people who wanted higher public spending that taxes must rise to pay for it, whereas if you told them the consequence was a mere delay in repaying the national debt, you would get the answer 'Why should we pay the debt? We didn't incur it; leave it to posterity.'[28] But against this political point, said Lowe, there was a strictly financial one with, however, even graver political implications. The lower the debt, the lower the interest on future borrowing. Because the debt had been so doggedly reduced since 1815, Britain could now borrow more cheaply than anyone else and, without wishing to disparage his Rt. Hon. Friends the Secretary for War and the First Lord of the Admiralty, 'I hold that [this] gives more strength to the country than the aggregate amount of our fleets and armies at any given moment.'[29]

In the ensuing debate Ward Hunt tried his hand at prediction again. With impressive precision, he opined that the malt duty would come off about 20 years after a compulsory education bill was passed, this being the lag needed for beer-drinkers, now properly instructed, to realise the tax fell on them.[30] There was some opposition to the tax on guns, but not from Stephen Cave who thought 'it would prevent idle boys living in villages from getting hold of old rusty guns at Easter and Christmas, wandering about the country, and shooting sometimes a sparrow, sometimes a cow and not infrequently themselves'.[31]

But the year was 1870, and Lowe was soon dealing with bigger guns.

II

Lowe had supported the Crimean War with enthusiasm. But, as Chancellor after 1868, his approach to military expenditure was simple: it must not be stinted when Britain's defence was at stake, but nothing should be left over for 'meddlesomeness' abroad. At the start of his Chancellorship, he offered a description of the government's principles in one word 'concentration . . . drawing our forces together to that one point where they will be rendered most available for the defence of the country instead of being scattered and rendered useless by being distributed all over the world'.[32]

So the spending should fit the threat, and initially Lowe saw the threat as Prussia. In February 1870 he warned the cabinet that

> There is one Power, too, that studiously keeps open a grievance with us, is almost contemptuous in its treatment of France, is perpetually encroaching and menaces the peace of the whole world.[33]

But when France declared war on Prussia in July 1870, Lowe changed his tune. When Gladstone responded by signing a new treaty guaranteeing Belgian neutrality, Lowe told him that Britain's 'obsession' with the Lowlands no longer made sense. And, although inclined to scoff at Bismarck's 'evidence' that Belgium had been in imminent danger from France, Lowe also found the allegation quite useful. Whether or not France had had designs on Belgium, the Prussian war would certainly have ended them. Lowe thus became the only man in the country to see the war as reason to *reduce* Britain's defence spending.[34]

And when Germany seized Alsace and Lorraine, Lowe's response was that 'modern', 'scientific' Germany had deserved her victory, the fall of Louis Napoleon was 'a clearing of the moral atmosphere' and 'lost French provinces' were no concern of Britain.[35] Furthermore, the Prussian victory showed that a standing army could be defeated by a nation 'whose troops have been called from the counter, the loom and the plough'.[36] Given that standing armies pushed governments into war whereas civilians liable to be called up would resist any war other than a defensive one, this was a heartening lesson for liberals everywhere. Lowe lost little time in sending Gladstone some detailed plans for replacing a large part of the proposed increase in Army numbers by a civilian militia.[37]

But Gladstone had already resolved to restore the Army, as quickly as possible, to the size at which he had found it in 1868. There was also to be a hasty update of armaments. Lowe briefly contemplated resignation, then swiftly went ahead and raised the £2¼ million required, plus the £750,000 bill for the abolition of purchase of military commissions – a price which Lowe, at any rate, was hardly going to begrudge paying.

The need to raise revenue now mated fruitfully with Lowe's taste for providing a shock. A few months previously he had written to Lady Salisbury that:

> I shall have to put on some new tax: what is your particular taste in the matter? Don't say income tax, for any fool can do that. I want something more recherche. My whole attention has been fixed on the taking off of taxes, and I never meant to put any on so I am caught unprepared.[38]

Politicians in Lowe's day possessed no researchers or think-tanks to think up brilliant and silly ideas. Lowe did however have Jevons, and his new pamphlet *The Match Tax, A Problem in Finance*. And a match tax, to solve a problem in finance, Lowe proceeded to impose.

By putting ½d. on each box of 100 wooden matches, double if they were made of wax, Lowe told the Commons he could raise £550,000 per year. The tax would be cheap to collect, hard to evade. It had the advantage that everyone would pay it – an important step towards the day when every member of the community contributed according to their means. 'I think every man, above the actual pauper, should be called upon to contribute something towards the government of the country.'[39]

So far, Lowe was barely knee-deep in the contentious waters he loved. But this he soon remedied. Yes, some in the match industry might lose their jobs, but they had the blessing of easy mobility, conferred on them by lack of fixed capital. To the charge that the match tax interfered with industry and deranged trade, Lowe retorted, 'Of course it does' because any tax did.[40] This was in itself provocative. Even on the first estimates, the tax represented an *ad valorem* duty of over 100 per cent. (The match firm Bryant and May were eventually to win the contest with a prediction of 500 per cent.) No one except Lowe thought the match tax was comparable with, for instance, the increase in sugar duty needed to bring in the same revenue.

And almost no one came to Lowe's defence. Disraeli, who knew that match-sellers had the kind of grip on popular sentiment that nurses were to attain in the late twentieth century, predicted mass destitution in the match industry. Henry Fawcett damned the tax as offending every canon of Adam Smith, whose disciple Lowe professed himself to be. Fawcett confessed he 'did not pretend to have the slightest knowledge of naval and military affairs',[41] a statement which commanded the House's assent, and no doubt the reason why he fell back on the traditional nostrum of cutting out (unspecified) waste in the Army and Navy as a way of getting no new taxes *and* better defence. All Lowe had for support were the likes of George Anderson, Liberal MP for Glasgow who thought 'the sooner they had some disagreeable tax the better for the country, for it might arouse people to a sense of the iniquitous scale on which tax was levied'.[42] Lowe's attempt to invoke public safety – the tax would stop 'idle boys throwing lighted matches onto loose straw'[43] – set off a tiny class war when Dilke said it was the rich who were careless with matches.[44] This was too much for Dr Donald Dalrymple, Liberal MP for Bath, who knew for a fact that 'in the agricultural districts, when a poor woman had little food to give her children to keep them quiet she would frequently give them four or five matches to play with'.[45] Even *The Economist*, whose editorial started by endorsing anything 'which makes the more numerous class of society – collectively a very wealthy class – pay any part of the taxation' reluctantly concluded the tax was not practicable because of the damage to the export trade in matches: a rare slip-up on their part, as Lowe had specifically exempted exports.[46]

Even in the cabinet Lowe was isolated. When he first became Chancellor, Gladstone had advised him to put as much as possible through the cabinet first, to bind it with its own complicity.[47] It was sound enough counsel on the public spending side; as long as balancing the budget was an agreed aim, each minister would check his colleagues' largesse in case the cost fell on him. But it was an essential precept when it came to raising revenue, and Lowe was now going to pay a heavy price for ignoring it over the match tax.

However, Lowe's most effective adversary – the only one to add action to words – was the one most closely affected. Bryant and May were to become famous in industrial history for the match-makers' strike of 1888, when they faced mass demonstrations by their workers, and enabled Cardinal Manning to pioneer the trade of industrial conciliator. But on this occasion the workers were demonstrating with, not against, their firm.

On 24 April a letter from Bryant and May appeared in *The Times*. It began with a rebuttal of Lowe's claim to be on the side of safety. On the contrary, said Bryant and May, 'price with the millions, to whom farthings are of importance, will carry the day and nine-tenths of the matches sold will be of the very commonest description'.[48] (They were better economists than Lowe: a flat rate tax on all types of match will, always provided the consumers are rational economic men, produce an income effect but no substitution effect, that is, make them buy cheaper matches.) Above all, Lowe provoked the match firm's wrath by the light-hearted comments which had accompanied the tax, first saying that he was going to 'present this tax to America as a tribute to my admiration of her finance' (the US already had a match tax) and then saying matchboxes in future ought to carry the motto 'ex luce lucellum' (from light a small profit).[49]

No doubt some, maybe even some match-girls, preferred Lowe's clever pun to Disraeli's practised tears. Be that as it may, on the same day as their letter, Bryant and May opened the forcible side of their campaign, with a demonstration during which the police had to persuade Lowe to hide in the subway under the Palace of Westminster. The next day he announced that he was withdrawing the entire budget.

The reaction to the match tax alone, however ferocious, would hardly have led the government to this extreme step. But almost as unpopular in the Commons were his proposals to double the succession duty where a son inherited his father's estate, and to decimalise the standard rate of income tax.[50]

Estate duty currently varied inversely with the closeness of the tie, direct descendants paying 1 per cent. Lowe proposed to double this, a measure which, to *The Times*, violated every sympathy of common humanity, and would more than double the rate of evasion into the bargain.[51] As for calculating income tax on a percentage basis, this, Lowe explained, was designed to give the Treasury exactly the revenue it needed. There had been too many occasions recently when a penny on or off income tax was too much but no change was too little. Critics might have retorted the problem was of Lowe's own making. Previous Chancellors had fine-tuned by changing the rate half-way through the fiscal year: by collecting the whole tax in January Lowe had closed this option down. Instead, however, the main attack was on the temptation a continuous scale would put in the Treasury's way whenever it was short of money. Gloomy predictions were made of a ratchet effect leading into the realms of chronic extravagance.

It was Lowe who withdrew the budget. But it was Gladstone who announced its replacement – twopence on income tax. In some quarters this was every bit as unpopular. Even the penny added to income tax in the original budget had prompted *The Times* to note that the Cassandra of the Reform Bill, who had warned so eloquently of 'a race for popularity' in which 'everything would be sacrificed to the proletariat' was now leading the race himself.[52] Disraeli complained that, under the Liberals, indirect taxes were now down and direct ones up. W.H. Smith calculated that four-fifths of income tax payers earned less than £300 a year; most faced a harder struggle against poverty than the artisan or working man, both blessedly free from the need to keep up 'what was termed "a decent and respectful appearance"'.[53] Nor could Smith find a precedent for raising income taxes without a war or the threat of one.

One alternative, of course, would have been to allow the national debt to rise. In fact Lowe could have raised his £3 million simply by suspending the reduction of the debt currently taking place by the conversion of undated government stock into terminable annuities. When Gladstone implied such a suspension would be the start of the road to ruin, he was reminded that not only was the terminable annuities scheme his brainchild, but he had introduced it in 1866 with the specific recommendation that, unlike the old sinking fund, it could be suspended when necessary. When Lowe said suspension would be breaking a compact, *The Times* asked how the nation could break a compact with itself.[54]

The match-tax debacle did nothing to change Lowe's basic fiscal canons. There was no reason why it should have. He continued to oppose new exemptions and cut down existing ones. Indeed, in both the budget struck down and its replacement, Lowe made it clear he would have liked all exemptions to go. He knew of no proper exemptions from taxes, he said, except in those cases where taxes were not worth collecting: 'No exemptions ought to be allowed unless the public would be losers by the taxation.'[55] But why pursue this line of thought, Lowe sighed, why go into it in any detail when 'I do not suppose the [House] would assist me in doing away with these exemptions.'[56]

Reassurance like this was not enough for the landed interest, who remained convinced that Lowe was out to remove tax concessions they saw not as privileges but as the only fair basis for agriculture. One MP worked out with horror that Lowe would see no distinction between a bequest of land and a gift 'to supply petticoats to the widows of evangelical negroes'.[57] This seems excessive, since all Lowe was refusing was the right of agricultural horses and carts (exempt from duty because they worked) to take their owners to church once a week. How, Lowe asked members opposite, was the Inland Revenue going to prove that a man out with his horse and cart on a Sunday *wasn't* going to church?[58]

But Liberal MPs' dominant feeling by now was reluctance to throw out a second Liberal budget, and the measures went through. Not everyone was surprised when the figures for 187½ showed them to have been unnecessary: Lowe could have cancelled both budgets and still achieved a small fiscal surplus. Indeed Liberals kept up the pressure for a more relaxed fiscal policy for much of 1871, giving Lowe another chance to campaign for debt reduction rather than tax reduction. This time, instead of praising low interest rates as a better asset than fleets and armies, he stressed how much easier low interest rates made it to *buy* fleets and armies. In his budget he had raised taxes to pay for increased military and naval spending. Now (replying to yet another call to suspend repayment and cut taxes instead) he rebuked Sir Tollemache Sinclair for suggesting that the debt could be left alone to shrink, as a proportion of national income, in the sun of economic growth. That, said Lowe, was what foolish people had said on the eve of the Napoleonic Wars, and the dangers were greater now than then. Look at what France was having to borrow to pay the 'tribute' Prussia now demanded, and the interest she would have to pay as a result of running up peacetime deficits as recommended by Sir Tollemache. As for another MP's demand that priority go to cutting duties which pressed heavily on the working class – tea, sugar and coffee – no one would benefit more from a lower debt than the working class themselves. Lowe finished on a crescendo which had the effect of reminding the House that, on occasion, he could wrap his policy in virtue and history even more rousingly than Gladstone himself. Above all, he told Members, they should remember that current prosperity was the result of a long course of self-denial by their forbears:

> Is it to be said that we are to come in for this rich inheritance and do nothing for our children?... It will not be believed that we are the children of the men of Trafalgar and Waterloo... if we sit down in luxury – English luxury, as it is now called in France – and do nothing whatever in the spirit of those who expended

> their blood and treasure to earn for us this prosperity and tranquillity which we now enjoy. In France, the idol of the nation is glory, and a miserable idol it is; but a worse idol than that is the individualism and selfishness which lead a man not to consider public questions with respect to the community of which he is a member [but] to be content to let others shift for themselves.[59]

Cutting the debt, furthermore, made war less likely in the first place. Potential enemies will inspect your interest rates with trepidation as well as awe.

> A high price of funds is a great source of national strength... It is an unanswerable witness to our honesty and prudence. It is also a silent threat. People are naturally shy of a contest with an adversary who can command the sinews of war at a rate so much cheaper than themselves. It is thus a very potent guarantee for peace.[60]

Lowe's position, therefore, was that sound finance was not just the source of a kind of national strength to be valued far above mere military success, but that it also guaranteed the only kind of military success that mattered, defence of your own realm.

As it was he began 1872, like 1870, with a huge surplus. Lowe's extreme caution was by now causing some grim amusement. Even four days from the end of the old fiscal year, he was estimating a surplus of £400,000 less than it turned out to be. (Because, for the first time, the budget was presented before the old fiscal year was over, it gave Lowe a double opportunity to underestimate the revenue.) The budget itself, *The Economist* complained, was uncharacteristically dull. The previous year's 2d. on income tax was taken off again, income tax allowances raised, the duty on coffee halved and that was more or less it. The result was that Lowe once again faced fierce criticism from his own side as well as the Tories. James White, a veteran champion of low taxes who had consistently outflanked Gladstone in his calls for economy, accused Lowe of irrational expectations. Ever since he had become Chancellor he had underestimated tax receipts, and was getting worse; his budget speech of 1871, where he 'turned his back on prosperity' and forecast depression in the forthcoming financial year, had been 'a specimen of ludicrous lugubriousness'. The revenue for 187½ showed that income tax need not have risen at all.[61]

We have seen Lowe's worries over Gladstone as a reckless Chancellor without proper plans. We have also seen James White and others rueing the tax cuts lost to Lowe's own hyper-caution at the Treasury. On the whole the charge stands, as Table 9.1 suggests.

Except for 1871, the pattern is monotonous in the extreme. Every year Lowe reported a surplus. Every year he projected a surplus without his proposed tax cuts and a balanced budget with. Every year the result was another large surplus. The year 1871 differed only insofar as it featured tax *increases* to achieve the inevitable forecast of a balanced budget, and the inevitable surplus as the actual outcome.

So the country was losing the full benefits of having an economiser at the Treasury; public-spending restraint was being translated less into tax reductions than into a string of 'accidental' surpluses. The arithmetical explanation lay in Lowe's habit, in the case of a large number of taxes, of simply making actual receipts for the current year (or, when not finalised, forecasts of actual receipts) the basis of his estimates for the coming one. When some 'elasticity' in the revenue was assumed, it was often implausibly small. For an economist who based so much of his fiscal philosophy on what would now be called 'supply-side economics' the incongruity was especially glaring.

But an arithmetical explanation of Lowe's 'accidental' errors is little use without a political explanation of the arithmetic. James Wilson was probably right when he thought Gladstone and Lowe

Table 9.1 Chancellor Lowe's balance sheet

Financial year	*Projected surplus with no budget changes* (£ million)	*Projected surplus with proposed budget changes* (£ million)	*Actual surplus* (£ million)
1869/70	3.350*	0.442	3.500
1870/1	4.327	0.330	2.311
1871/2	−2.713	0.007	2.815
1872/3	3.602	0.312	5.894
1873/4	4.741	0.291	0.869

* After change in timing of income tax receipts (0.032 without this).

were conspiring to sound pessimistic about the prospects of the revenue, knowing too well the flood of demands for extravagance that would follow if its true elasticity were conceded. Bagehot had a simpler explanation: Lowe's bad eyesight. Unable to absorb hundreds of columns of figures in small print, he had to ask his civil servants to summarise. Consciously or not, their parsimonious instincts infused what they gave him and so steered policy onto an unnecessarily timid path.

Lowe's final budget, in 1873, began with the unveiling of the by-now-expected unexpected surplus for the dying financial year. This time Lowe awarded himself especial plaudits: the surplus had been achieved despite a £1.5 million compensation payment to the US government over the *Alabama* case. (The *Alabama*, a Confederate commerce raider, had put out from a British port during the Civil War. After international arbitration, Britain had agreed to pay £3 million in two instalments.) Choosing his words with even less caution than usual, Lowe invited the House to share his hopes that the government would be asked to make similar payments in the future. What he meant was his approval of the process of international arbitration which had led to the settlement, not the settlement in itself. But his belated attempt to explain this had to struggle against the shouts of MPs who already thought the sum excessive and the process humiliating.

Lowe himself kept his temper, but not for long. The Tories' protests over the *Alabama* expenditure were a flea-bite compared with their demands on the other side of the balance sheet.

'Both Gladstone and Disraeli', Colin Matthew has said, 'saw government finance, and especially the great drama of the budget, the annually renewed social contract of the Victorian State, as the context in which [social and economic] relationships could be both fiscally and politically expressed'.[62] No one held such sentiments more strongly than Lowe. That was why, in the early 1860s, he had criticised Gladstone as a Chancellor eager to heap taxes onto the rich. The result, Lowe warned, would be class war. Now in 1873 he saw the threat to peace coming from those Conservatives who wanted to put more of the burden on the poor. For in the budget debate W.H. Smith proposed that, instead of Lowe's intended abolition of sugar duty, the available money be used to reduce local rates. Lowe proceeded to lose control of himself.

The government's guiding principle, said Lowe, was that cuts in direct taxes must be matched by cuts in indirect taxes. This alone could maintain justice for all. In this spirit he had cut income tax specifically because he was going to abolish the sugar duty. If the sugar duty remained then, far from lowering local rates as Smith proposed, he would have to reverse the cut in income tax. Smith, therefore, was forcing him to reconstruct the whole budget. But even this was not the worst: Smith had made his specific demand in the course of proposing his own motion 'that, before deciding on the further reduction of indirect taxation, it is desirable that the House should be put in possession of the views of the Government with reference to the maintenance of the argument of direct taxation, both imperial and local'.[63]

This caused Lowe even more offence than the specific proposal on sugar. If the House agreed to this motion, he said, it would be withdrawing its trust from the government and 'call[ing] on us, as persons suspected, to give an account of our own principles and conduct'.

> It is impossible to conceive a more decided, a more flaming insult to the Government than is contained in such a proposal ... it is my Budget not only technically but actually, it is not only my budget, but I am proud of it, and I mean to stand by it ... I should like to know ... what hon. Gentlemen opposite will do if this Vote of Censure is carried. That, however, is a subject so painful that I will not anticipate it ...[64]

The Conservatives, Lowe concluded in only a very slightly calmer spirit, were asking for a treble remission of taxes for the rich. They approved his proposed cut in income tax; they wanted lower rates instead of abolishing the sugar duty; and the wording of Smith's motion clearly implied some further cut in direct taxation was required 'before they will allow us to get at indirect taxation'. This was not only 'in the highest degree unequal and unjust' but unwise and dangerous.[65]

> Do hon. Gentlemen opposite suppose that, having put power into the hands of the lower classes, they will tamely submit to see taxation modified against the poor and in favour of the rich? What is their view of the character of the poor? Do they consider

> that the poor are saints or that they are idiots?... It was not for this that we have been endeavouring to economise the public money... We wished the rich to remain in possession of their riches and that there should be no heart-burning in the country; but we wished also that justice be done to the poor; and miserable indeed it would be to reflect after laboriously economising the public revenue, that it was to come to this at last.[66]

In fact, the class implications were less stark than Lowe was suggesting. The stylised picture whereby the rich paid direct taxes and the poor indirect, never very accurate, was now increasingly archaic (as Smith had rightly intimated in the budget debate of 1871).[67] Plenty of artisans were by now paying income tax, while the burden of the rates was now pressing even on the very poor. The working-class radicals now calling for the complete abolition of income tax might be in a minority, but were probably by now closer to standard working-class sentiment than were Lowe's old-fashioned simplicities.[68]

Moreover, Lowe's claim that a cut in the rates would benefit only the relatively rich underlines the absence from his speech (and, for that matter, Smith's) of any sign of awareness that the incidence of taxes may not fall entirely on those who actually pay them. And when Lowe did, occasionally, take up the issue of tax incidence, his analysis was not very assured even by the standards of the day. Twice he told the brewers to stop complaining about their licence duty because they could pass it on to the consumer: if the brewer 'could not help' paying the duty, equally the drinkers were paying him 'for things they must have'.[69] Of course, if Lowe literally meant he thought the demand for beer was unaffected by its price, he was correct in deducing that the consumer would shoulder the whole imposition. But it seems hardly likely that this is what he meant.

But Lowe had a second argument up his sleeve. You may dislike paying the licence, he told the brewers, but, so far as it reduces your profits, it deters entry to the trade until profits recover to their old level. If this is consolation for brewers, it is consolation for any trade, paying any level of tax. It is perhaps surprising, then, that Lowe did not use the argument on a wider constituency.[70]

Lowe's defence of the house tax also got him into some strange places once he started discussing its incidence. Opponents had damned the tax as regressive because its incidence fell not on the proprietor but on the tenant. In rebuttal, Lowe stated:

> As persons must inhabit houses, the demand for them could not be constrained; but the proprietor who did not want his houses to stand empty, must submit to accept such rents for them as were fixed by general competition.[71]

So demand for houses is inelastic. Does Lowe also see the supply of houses as inelastic? Surely not: he is not claiming that *no* proprietor would let his house stand empty (quite apart from the effect of the house tax on the supply of new houses). In effect, then, his 'rebuttal' *supports* the idea that the house tax falls on the tenant.

III

Lowe's final months as Chancellor were rendered unhappy by greater irritants than W.H. Smith. A shoal of small mismanagements was now snapping at the Treasury's reputation. That there were so many minor scandals was itself seen as a major scandal. And there were two major scandals in their own right.[72]

Disraeli had bought the telegraph for the nation in 1868. The civil servant who had handled the purchase, Frank Scudamore, was kept on by Lowe, to extend the telegraph into a full national system. In 1873 it emerged that Scudamore had overspent his budget by more than £600,000 and used workingmens' deposits in the Post Office Savings Bank to do so. No one alleged that Scudamore was personally corrupt, or that the depositors were in danger of losing their money, but Lowe was fiercely criticised for his almost non-existent supervision of Scudamore's activities. The government narrowly headed off a censure motion which Lowe insisted would have required his resignation, only for the Chancellor to plunge straight into a second communications scandal. Here the trouble had begun when the government offered the sultan of Zanzibar a mail service to link his kingdom with Aden and the Cape Colony. In return he was meant to suppress the local slave trade. Lowe took on himself the task of finding a company to handle the mail. Instead of putting it out to open tender, he offered the job to the Union Steamship

Company, sweetening the package by promising a renewal of their (much more profitable) west coast of Africa run. It then emerged that two rival companies had offered to do the Zanzibar service for less, and unconditionally at that. In the ensuing Commons debate it became all too obvious that Lowe had entirely forgotten about one of these offers.[73]

Lowe's reputation for competence had now descended precipitously. The match tax had turned out to be but the first step on the way down. Lowe himself now realised that he had become a liability to the government, at any rate in his existing position. A reshuffle was imminent anyway; Gladstone informed Lowe of 'the necessity of changing his office',[74] and Lowe wrote to Gladstone offering his resignation as Chancellor. In August 1873 he was transferred to the Home Office. His new responsibilities included electoral law and Gladstone, who took over the Treasury himself, was promptly and wrongly informed by Lowe that he must now submit himself for re-election in his constituency of Greenwich.[75]

IV

Bagehot's study of 'Mr Lowe as Chancellor' is an often shrewd portrait of Lowe's strengths and weaknesses. It must remain speculative whether, as Bagehot claims, Lowe's mind was already so full of other subjects that he had less 'free and applicable mind' to give to finance than other Chancellors did. But it is hard to dispute that Lowe, in Bagehot's words, never learned 'the way of putting an argument so as to suit the House of Commons'.[76] In particular, Lowe was incapable of meeting the requirement to be uninteresting. This was essential. Make it seem that 'the department has attended to the dreary detail' and parliament will leave everything, not just the dreary detail, to the department. But Lowe could not help being brilliant. Worse, much off his brilliance lay in his efflorescent mastery of general principles. 'He makes the dry bones live. He wraps them in illustrations which Macaulay might envy.' This made for enjoyable speeches but not successful ones. Parliamentary skill consisted of paring generalities to the minimum needed to support your particular point of the moment. 'By doing so you offend as few people as possible, you startle as few people as possible, and you expose yourself to as few people as possible.'[77] It almost sounds as if Bagehot thought Lowe longed to offend as few people as possible, and was barred from this pleasant goal only by lack of skill. But Bagehot must have known Lowe better than that.

Self-congratulation was not an experience Lowe ever found embarrassing, and when he left the Treasury in 1873 he told Lord Derby that his Chancellorship had been 'a great success... I am the first Finance Minister under the Reformed Parliament. It remains to be seen whether anyone else who does his duty will fare much better.'[78] Gladstone had just sent Lowe a unique end-of-term report, not so much on his performance as Chancellor as on the characteristics he had brought, and failed to bring, to the job. Echoing Bagehot, Gladstone saw the clarity and power of Lowe's mind as 'a difficulty and a danger' so far as they made him see everything in 'a burning, almost a scorching light'. A photographer had once shown a disbelieving Gladstone how his art worked best against a misty background: the light should be diffused and not concentrated. 'Is not your light too much concentrated? Does not its intensity darken the surroundings?' and especially other persons, a danger when 'our profession obliges us constantly to deal with persons'.[79] After that the mood lightened as Gladstone went on to congratulate Lowe on his justified unpopularity, a sure sign of financial competence:

> I could easily name the two worst chancellors of the exchequer of the last forty years; against neither of whom did I ever hear a word while they were in (I might almost add, nor for them after they were out)... Of course, I do not say that this necessity of being unpopular should induce us to raise our unpopularity to the highest point.[80]

But Gladstone's tone changed abruptly after Lowe went to Sheffield to tell the annual Feast of Master Cutlers about his own splendid performance at the Treasury. 'So far as relieving you from taxation is concerned' said Lowe, 'I believe you would seek in vain in British history for anything like what has been done during these last few years.' By contrast, the accusations against him of the last few months were 'matters so insignificantly small that they are not worth a thought'.[81]

Lowe apologised to his audience for bringing all this into an after-dinner speech. On the contrary, sniffed the *Pall Mall Gazette*, if Lowe wanted to vindicate himself, a 'Budget speech' to Sheffield cutlers over their claret was almost the only safe way to do it.[82] The *Gazette*'s metropolitan readers no doubt enjoyed this comment, but not Gladstone, who retorted that a Chancellor's first duty was to look after public expenditure and here Lowe had been 'wretchedly deficient'.[83]

Of all the comments which stung this sensitive and touchy man at the end of his Chancellorship, the charge that he had failed to get a grip on public spending was the one that hurt most. Was it fair?

In Ward Hunt's last year at the Treasury total public spending was £74.972 million. In Lowe's final year it was £76.466 million. If we remove the Abyssinia (Hunt) and Ashanti (Lowe) war expenditure, together with the Alabama compensation payment, the increase over Lowe's Chancellorship rises to £2.497 million. If debt service is excluded it falls marginally to £2.409 million. If Indian expenditure is believed to be largely beyond the Treasury's control and excluded too, the margin narrows again slightly, to £2.363 million. It looks as if, whichever way you read the figures, Gladstone has a point.

But how much of the increase could have been prevented? Lowe himself had just been telling a select committee of the House of Commons how hard it was to keep expenditure down. When James White (again) asked him if it was a 'popular delusion' that the Treasury had direct control over what other departments spent, Lowe retorted that he did not know if it was popular, but it was certainly a delusion.

> I can remonstrate, and if not attended to, I can appeal to the Cabinet. You can prevent casual expenditure, and make their lives uneasy, but nothing more.

However even this was much better than nothing:

> The Chancellor of the Exchequer, if he makes a little remonstrance, and gives good reasons for it, very often works out in the end what he wants. There is a moral suasion exercised.[84]

And clearly Lowe thought his moral suasion had worked. The Sheffield speech answered in advance Gladstone's charge that he had been 'wretchedly deficient'. Take off all the expenditure which brings in revenue (the post office, telegraphs, crown land), said Lowe, and you had a £2-million cut in public spending during his Chancellorship. Take off all 'necessary' increases (education, prisons, police and health) and the cut exceeded £3 million. And this was despite a number of instances where he had been 'liberal in the extreme . . . If you look at the Fine Arts I have spent £8000 buying Sir Robert Peel's pictures and £50,000 on splendid collections of antiquity for the British Museum'.[85]

This last boast did nothing to mollify the unhappy Sir Henry Cole, whose indignation finally boiled over. He took the occasion of the opening of a school of art in Spitalfield to declare that the late Chancellor had 'a flinty bosom', was 'a wilful man', 'a man of very bad judgement', 'no statesman whatever' and, puzzlingly, 'a milk-and-water Rabelais'. Loftily, the *Spectator* reminded him that 'in politics, temper never pays'.[86]

But on the broader picture he had painted, Lowe would get the support of Sydney Buxton in his magisterial 1888 study of Victorian public finance. Lowe, alone among Chancellors, had two chapters to himself, 'Prosperity' and 'Adversity'. The reversal was meant to be in Lowe's own fortunes, not in the state of the economy, yet much of Buxton's comparison turns on the fall in public spending until 1871 and its climb back thereafter, a point more recently echoed by Jonathan Parry.[87] But, taking the record overall, Buxton, like Lowe, put fiscally productive and/or non-preventable increases in public spending at £3 billion, underlined Gladstone's own support for each of the 'non-preventables', and concluded that, so far as Lowe had discretion, he brought about a reduction of more than £500,000.[88]

It was on defence spending, however, that Gladstone was particularly dissatisfied with Lowe. Indeed at times he felt ranged against not just Lowe, but the rest of his cabinet – an experience he would repeat just before his final resignation in 1894. Months after the 1871 budget had added £2 million to defence spending, Gladstone was urging Lowe to take it off again.[89] But Lowe gave Gladstone little help. In December 1871 Gladstone recorded a cabinet in which 'for 2½ hours we discussed Army estimates, mainly on reduction, and the C of E did not speak one word'.[90] The next month Gladstone told Lowe 'we are I fear drifting straight on the rocks as we did last year' and was 'at a loss to conceive' how £400,000 was now being put about as the maximum retrenchment possible.[91] The following November he told Goschen that for two years he had 'given in considerably to the rest of the Cabinet', but now the calmer international situation was 'impossible for alarmism to overlook or misapprehend'.[92] But between 1871 and 1873, combined military and naval spending fell by the despised £400,000 only, a reduction of 1.6 per cent. Here, undoubtedly, was the gravamen of the charge that Lowe had been 'wretchedly deficient'. All the same, the charge is a ludicrous one and why it has been uncritically accepted ever since[93] is itself a minor historical mystery. Over the period of Lowe's Chancellorship as a whole (1868–73), defence spending fell by 5 per cent overall, by 18 per cent per head of population at constant prices, and by 24 per cent in terms of its share of national income.[94] If this is wretched deficiency, what Gladstonian but Gladstone himself would not clamour for more of it?

Certainly Gladstone, in his own brief Chancellorship in 1873/4, showed no signs of being able to do any better himself. His proposed budget of 1874 included provision for a £600,000 cut in combined Army and navy estimates. Negotiation with the two ministers concerned failed to find any serious savings at all; and, as Matthew[95] (1982) shows, it was this deadlock that pushed Gladstone into dissolving parliament, losing the election, installing the first majority Conservative government for 28 years, and aborting the last ever proposal (to date) to abolish income tax.

How the end of income tax, had Gladstone carried it through, would have affected the balance between direct and indirect taxation is unclear, since Gladstone never finalised the details of how he was to fill the gap. Lowe's own Chancellorship, taken over all, left the balance undisturbed. Indeed the whole period 1855–80 was a long punctuation mark in the massive shift from indirect to direct taxation between 1832 and 1914. In the 1840s and 1850s tariffs were being reduced, and income tax used as an ostensible stopgap until the tariff remissions paid for themselves by stimulating increased trade. Gladstone's great budget of 1853 switched the focus from reduction to abolition of tariffs and, for all his stated hope that income tax would be gone by 1860, cemented it into place as a permanent feature of the fiscal landscape. And, while most Conservatives continued to worry about direct taxes more than most Liberals, both sides were reasonably content with the 'settlement' of 1853. Certainly the long stasis he inherited helped Lowe to articulate a consensus which neither W.H. Smith nor the Liverpool Financial Reform Association (who wanted an end to all excise duties) were going to be allowed to disturb.[96]

As for the overall level of taxation, Lowe benefited from prosperity during his term. It is worth stressing how very favourable the figures were. Between 1868 and 1873, output averaged 6.6 per cent annual growth in nominal terms and 5.0 per cent in real. The corresponding figures for output per head were 5.6 and 4.0 per cent, respectively. It was, naturally, the growth in total real output (beaten only by 1861–6 and 1884–9 of five-year periods between 1850 and 1914) which helped Lowe's finances the most, but the gentle inflation of the period also brought in a modest degree of fiscal drag. As for 1871, the year about which Lowe had such forebodings, it was, in each of the measures save real output per head, the best year of the lot.[97] Lowe's attribution of the buoyant revenue to his own handling of the economy need not be scorned altogether; lower taxes are good for growth whether tax freedom day occurs in June or, as in Lowe's time, early in February. In any case to achieve £12.5-million tax cuts and pay off £36 million of the national debt – a higher annual rate than any government since 1815 – is pretty good Gladstonian finance and bears comparison with any of Gladstone's four Chancellorships.

Shortly before Lowe's move to the Home Office in 1873, he, Ayrton and Gladstone had been satirised by W.S. Gilbert. In *The Happy Land*, Prime Minister, Chancellor and Commissioner of Works performed a can-can while they sang of their devotion to economy and – in a kind of trial run for Gilbert's *Iolanthe* – lectured the inhabitants of fairyland for their extravagantly dear (and artistically terrible) statues and temples. Gilbert was right only insofar that there was little to choose between Lowe and Gladstone in their successes and failures in public economy. But a rival artistic verdict on Lowe's Chancellorship came from Lowe himself, albeit in verse well below his usual standard:

> Twelve million of Taxes I struck off
> Left behind me six million of gains
> Of Debt forty million I shook off
> And got well abused for my pains.[98]

10
Joining the 'Europe' and Shrinking the Pound

As Chancellor of the Exchequer after 1868, Lowe, like other Chancellors before 1914 (and after 1997), assumed no direct responsibility for monetary matters. The framework in which he operated was the Bank Charter Act of 1844. This restricted the issue of notes by the Bank of England to the equivalent of its gold and silver reserves plus £14 million, and represented a belated victory for the Currency School, associated with Ricardo, whose theories implied that such a rule was both necessary and sufficient for a stable volume of credit. As Chancellor, however, Lowe was drawn into the debate over whether Britain should join a European currency union.

Despite a broad coalition of curmudgeons – the remnants of the Chartists, Carlyle (of course), the reactionary MP Colonel Sibthorp and the xenophobic edge of the middle class – the Great Exhibition of 1851 had been a joyful event. Having goods from so many countries on display, however, it did highlight the difficulty of identifying good value when each article was priced in a different currency. Manufacturers, merchants and Chambers of Commerce had learnt this lesson many times over by 1865, the year France, Belgium, Italy and Switzerland established a common coinage (the Latin Monetary Union). This fell well short of the European Union's post-1999 experiment. Member states continued to issue their own coins, and only fellow-members' governments (not their central banks) were obliged to accept them. The absence of penalties for suspending convertibility meant in effect that members could issue, and over-issue, paper money as and when they pleased. Convergence criteria and stability pacts were unheard of. None of this stopped the French politician and economist Felix Esquirou de Parieu calling for a single European currency, the 'europe', within a 'European Union' which would be run by a 'European Commission' and overseen by a 'European Parliament'.[1] And the following year the French government convened a conference of 20 countries to see the way to a more general common currency. Austria, Russia, Prussia, Turkey and the USA were among those who went along, while in Britain the Treasury 'saw no reason to decline' the invitation.[2]

The conference eventually recommended that any currency union must have a single (i.e. not bimetallic) gold standard, that its gold coins should have a uniform 90 per cent of fine metal in their composition, and that they should be denominated as 5 francs and multiples thereof. Lord Derby's Conservative government then set up a Royal Commission to investigate whether Britain should join in.

Expert witnesses were divided. Businessmen were almost unanimously in favour. Sir Louis Mallet, the indestructible voice of Cobdenism at the Board of Trade, said only a single unit of account would give exporters the full advantages of free trade, but thought it important to keep the Queen's head on British-minted coins. It was, as ever, the economists who were sharply split. Jevons was enthusiastic for a common currency, Newmarch against, Bagehot in favour if and only if the government decimalised the silver and copper coinage at the same time, while Goschen came down decisively for the 'don't knows'.[3]

This last was only after Goschen had offered a long and cogent analysis of the proposal to replace the pound with a 'new pound' worth 25 francs. As it happened, the pound was currently worth about 25.2 francs. The 25-franc sovereign would thus have to contain about 1 per cent less gold than the existing ones.

Some of the Commission, notably J.B. Smith MP, saw no problem with this; indeed they managed to make a virtue out of it. One thing that would have to be standardised in a common currency area was the charge for minting coin out of bullion. Britain currently, and uniquely, did this for nothing, and could consequently expect to start coining money for the whole union, and paying for the privilege, unless a common rule was agreed. But the proportionate charge currently made by the French Mint happily corresponded to the difference in value between the existing pound and the 'new' one. In other words, charging the French rate for minting new pounds would raise their value to that of the old ones. Gresham's Law would stall in its tracks, and both coins could co-exist happily in circulation.

Goschen took issue with this. No mintage charge, he said, could alter the fact that the 'new pound' would contain less gold than the old. The only fair basis for its introduction was a complete recoinage of the gold sovereign, and an appropriate, legally enforced, surcharge on debts taken out in the old currency. Jevons agreed all this was necessary, but thought it a cost well worth paying. A recoinage was overdue anyway, he said, while adding 2d. in the pound to all debts was essentially no different to putting 2d. in the pound on income tax. But when he came to the positive advantages of a common currency, Jevons put up a dire performance. Pinned down by J.G. Hubbard MP, a former governor of the Bank of England, as to the meaning of some windy remarks about 'the great general improvement in currencies' that monetary union would produce, he was unable to define, let alone quantify, the advantage of which he was speaking. Of his two specific arguments for a common currency, he admitted himself that the convenience to travellers was a minor consideration, stressing instead that 'our merchants will have the means of exactly estimating the value of goods or any money, in any part of the world whatever', and that if the pound were equated to the 25-franc piece, these merchants would easily make currency conversions in their heads.[4] Hubbard pounced. In that case, he inquired, what would 23 lb of a good at 2s. 8½d. per lb cost in French money? 'I am not prepared to say', replied Jevons. 'I am very bad at mental arithmetic.'[5]

The unimpressive performance by the only economist witness wholeheartedly for a common currency may have helped dictate the Commission's sceptical tone when it reported. The list of advantages it cited are straight out of the early twenty-first century. Greater price transparency would save time and trouble. Some small firms, currently deterred from trading abroad at all, would begin competing at import and export. Prices on both these fronts would thus fall, benefiting consumers and the labour market alike. The convenience to travellers passing through different countries was 'too obvious to require remark', while the dangers of *not* being part of any currency union must be recognised.[6] Not only would insiders tend to trade with each other, switching their trade away from outsiders, but there was a political dimension too:

> England has been forward in urging the policy of free trade on continental nations, and while her joining any movement originated abroad for promoting and facilitating commercial intercourse would be most favourably received, and would increase her influence among them, her declining to enter upon it might appear to be inconsistent with her general conduct upon such questions.[7]

Could Britain, in short, afford not to be at the heart of Europe?

These were solid advantages. So why did the Commission come down against British membership? In the first place, they considered the transparency arguments greatly overrated unless currency union were accompanied by metrication and decimalisation, two issues specifically placed outside their terms of reference. Secondly, like Goschen, they took the implications of replacing the pound with a 25-franc piece very seriously and, unlike Jevons, were not prepared to shrug off as minor inconveniences a general recoinage and legal coercion to change the terms of all existing debts. Their final verdict – that Britain should reject the franc and instead everyone else should adopt the pound – shines out as all the more perverse in consequence. If other countries adopted sterling, said the Commission, they would admittedly undergo the inconveniences which had just been pronounced unacceptable to Britain. But foreigners, luckily, were used to this kind of thing:

> we cannot but think, however, that the difficulty and inconvenience of a change would be less serious and less felt where the existing system is of a comparatively recent date, or is one in which changes have already taken place, within no distant period of time.[8]

II

In December 1868 Jevons published a long article on international coinage in the *Journal of the Statistical Society of London*. Here he greatly expanded his remarks to the Royal Commission, dismissed its objections to a common currency as either imaginary or pieces of nationalist prejudice and recanted on the idea of a complete recoinage, now arguing that it would not be necessary: sovereigns lightened by wear and tear would do admirably as 25-franc pieces as they stood.

Jevons thus seemed to want to melt down the 'good' money and keep the 'bad', a foretaste of the consistent lack of political judgement the europhile camp would show throughout the debate. Enemies of the 'europe' would adeptly pillory its friends – and especially Lowe himself, as we shall see – as out to defraud the nation by devaluing its currency. Lord Overstone had already gone on to the attack and, while Jevons' article never mentions him by name, much of it reads as a response to Overstone's theory of value and the defence of the existing, undiminished pound he had built on it.

Anyone who held gold coin, Overstone had said, had the right to melt it down and sell it. No amount of sleight-of-hand via mintage charges could alter the fact such people would now receive 1 per cent less gold than before. If a country with a paper currency suddenly announced that its notes would exchange for less gold, the fraud would be blatant and universally condemned. What Jevons and his friends were proposing came to exactly the same thing; indeed the new, smaller sovereign would acquire some of the characteristics of paper money. By exchanging for more than the value of gold it contained, it became a 'monster', part token, part commodity.[9]

So what? was the essence of Jevons' response. 'There is no such thing as value intrinsic in a thing... in an economical sense, the values of two things merely express the ratio in which they do as a fact exchange for each other.'[10] If the Mint sets 100 ounces of gold as the price of 99 ounces of coin this will fix their relative values. Should this not correspond to subjective values, one or the other will be in excess supply until it does. As for individuals being 'robbed' when they melt coin into bullion, said Jevons, it was a cardinal virtue of an international currency that people would no longer have to do this, as the sovereign became acceptable abroad as well as at home.

Jevons reiterated J.B. Smith's point that recoinage and mintage would dovetail so as to make the new sovereign worth as much as the old. He even seemed to say that a legal upgrading of debts would not after all be necessary: 'all inconvenience or injustice arising from the change in the sovereign might be entirely avoided by the imposition of a seignorage, or mint charge, equal in amount to the value of the gold subtracted'.[11]

In the second half of 1869 Overstone replied to these arguments in the course of two 'Papers on Gold Coinage'. To make purchasing power the standard was confused and confusing: purchasing power was irrelevant. 'The quantity of gold to which the Creditor is entitled is absolute – it does not depend on anything so uncertain and variable as the purchasing power of gold.'[12] Overstone accepted that gold coin, as an alternative to gold bullion, might be seen as the standard of value, but if so any mintage charge 'must be rigidly limited by the real cost of coinage'. Anything above this and 'the coin . . . wholly changes its character – it becomes a Token coin'. Moreover, once seignorage was accepted, what were to be the limits on it? 'Why not deduct 10 per cent or 50 per cent of the gold in the coin?'[13]

The gulf between Jevons' and Overstone's notions of value was as wide as ever. But Overstone's concession – that a smaller sovereign was acceptable so long as it was shrunk by no more than the cost of coining it – was a damaging one. The Master of the Mint had already estimated that mintage costs more than covered the shrinkage of the pound to 25-franc proportions. The research was by Jevons, who had actually worked in a Mint.[14] The conclusion was seized on by Lowe in a memorandum he sent the cabinet in June 1869. Here, however, the 'europe' made a decidedly oblique entry as Lowe put the case for a mintage charge, merely noting along the way that this would be a necessary condition for joining any international currency scheme. But he left his cabinet colleagues in no doubt of where he stood:

> it is highly probable, from the rapid progress that it is making all over the world, that one system of coinage will within no distant period be almost universally adopted, from which it will be impossible for great Britain to stand aloof.[15]

At the end of July, Lowe told the French government that Britain could join no monetary union that did not adopt the gold standard.[16] In parliament a few days later he responded to a speech by J.B. Smith MP, who had added a much more enthusiastic personal rider to the Commission's report. Smith now compared his continental tour of 1844, when he had had to change his money 14 times, with a recent trip to Italy when he had to change it just once. Was it not time for 'a common identical unit of account known to all the world, in the same way as notes representing musical sound could be interpreted by any musician, no matter what his nationality?'[17]

Replying, Lowe approved the idea in principle, but put forward three tests that would have to be passed before Britain could join. Would France abandon her bimetallic standard? Could the weight and fineness of British and European coins be standardised? Finally, could the national mints involved agree on a common charge for minting coin from bullion brought in by the public? The onus, again, appeared to be on the rest of Europe to adapt to British ways.

> I think it very probable, if France would meet us in this way... we might come to some arrangement by which we should get the blessing of one coinage throughout Europe, a great step in civilisation.[18]

Placing the burden on France in this way was particularly striking, given that Lowe had moments earlier proclaimed that France was right to charge its citizens for coining bullion, and Britain wrong not to: 'this useless piece of generosity', as Adam Smith had called it. Lowe went on to cite the further authority of J.S. Mill and McCulloch, but then unwisely parted company with Jevons. A complete recoinage and a mintage charge, Lowe opined, would *do away with* the need to write up all debts by law; gold coins by any criterion of value would be worth as much as in the past. The *bullion* they contained would be worth less, as they were smaller, but this was all to the good as it would stop people melting them down.[19]

The Times now stepped in. Unwilling to be too harsh on its former leader-writer, but sounding particularly English for the occasion, it complained that

> the embarrassing word 'value' – most absurd of economic terms occurs much too often in his exposition, while 'currency', 'seignorage', 'double standard', 'balance of exchanges' and other well-known occasions of despair chase one another through the columns devoted to the report of his speech.[20]

It is not clear exactly which monetary terms, if any, *The Times* would have allowed in a debate about money, but it did extract an assurance from Lowe the following day that 'I do not know what "intrinsic" value means... As far as I know there is no such thing as intrinsic value.'[21] But the 'europhiles' were now badly split. Smith thought neither a recoinage nor the legal writing up of debts was needed; Lowe was now advocating the former and Jevons the latter. Politically, Lowe's position was the least tenable of the three. Opponents swiftly cast him as the author of a reckless, economically illiterate plan to defraud the Englishman of his savings. 'The Chancellor of the Exchequer must be taught Political Economy' was the headline in the *Morning Advertiser*, which went on to call Lowe a 'chartered libertine' uttering 'great absurdity'.[22] If Lowe had miscalculated politically it was, paradoxically, from his conviction that legal tampering with debts would have been seen as the real interference with the value of the pound. As it was he found himself facing violent opposition in cabinet as well as in the country at large. To Cardwell, the secretary for war, Lowe responded that Jevons was right. All value was exchange value and, in the case of money, exchange value depended on quantity not quality. Lowe drew on Jevons' census of worn and lightweight sovereigns to argue that value could not reside in quantity of gold. If it did, then

> The nuisance of our system would be utterly unbearable, and no one could give or receive change without a pair of scales to determine the amount of depreciation... It follows from this fact that there is no necessary connection between the determination of the weight of the sovereign and its depreciation.[23]

The underlining was Gladstone's, after Cardwell had forwarded Lowe's memorandum with the comment that an Englishman in Paris, pocketing English dividends, would hardly see it that way when he started getting less gold.[24] Gladstone replied that 'I am also in favour of a mint charge but am no f.a. to Lowe and I am astonished.'[25] Exactly what astonished him is unclear, and after this the issue seems to have died down at cabinet level.[26] In February 1870 Lowe told the Commons that his first test for membership of a common currency had not been passed. France seemed unable to resolve on a single gold standard, so that 'the matter must stand over until the French government shall have arrived at a conclusion on that all-important subject'.[27]

Holding out against a common currency had many advantages, not least the fact that the Latin Monetary Union was due to renounce the gold standard in 1874 as unattainable. But it would also save Lowe much work, for he had now combined the Chancellor's office with that of Master of the Mint. This would save a public salary, he told the Commons, before proceeding to look at the much greater saving of abolishing the Mint altogether, and contracting out the manufacture of coins. In the end Lowe concluded, in faintly pre-Coasian fashion, that getting someone else to make the coins and checking their performance cost more than minting them yourself. Indeed Lowe extended the Mint's work to coinage for other countries, brushing aside the protests from MPs for Birmingham, where such coinage was being done privately.[28]

As the issues of the Mint and the European currency indicate, Lowe's monetary thinking was apt to emerge in a slightly random fashion, depending on the topical questions of the day and what sort of attention they were getting in parliament. The politician who did the most to elicit Lowe's opinions was anything but a serious figure – James Delahunty, the MP for Waterford.

In 1869 Delahunty proposed that £1 notes be prohibited in Ireland (as they were in England and Wales, though not in Scotland). This he advanced on the peculiar grounds that their existence caused a shortage of total 'monetary circulation' (not just gold). This scarcity was holding back manufacturing and destroying jobs.[29]

On the contrary, said Lowe, it was the removal of £1 notes which would damage industry: 'the results would be most harsh and cruel'. There was also the difficulty of Irish distrust of the gold sovereign – understandable, given how many of them were of less than standard weight. 'I understand that in out-of-the-way parts of that country they take 6d. off the sovereign in giving change [Sir Frederick Heygate: A shilling].'[30] The main interest of Lowe's speech, however, was his contention that England would do better to copy Ireland than the other way round. Indeed he went further, repeating the arguments for a gold-exchange standard that he had already put in the case of India.[31]

On the strength of this, Delahunty rather oddly withdrew his motion. It seems, though, that Lowe had planted a seed somewhere since three years later Delahunty was back, this time blaming Ireland's troubles on too *few* banknotes. He now wanted the government to suspend the Act of 1845 which had limited the number of joint-stock banks in Ireland, until their note issue per head of population matched that of Scotland. Lowe refused. Banks, he said, were not the cause of the wealth of nations. 'A country had Banks because it was rich. It was not necessarily rich because it had Banks.'[32] Again Delahunty withdrew, albeit less graciously than before:

> Mr DELAHUNTY said that after the miserable speech of the Chancellor of the Exchequer he was determined to bring forward this subject again next session, when he would smash him up.[33]

III

But none of this was at cabinet level. On the demise of the 'europe' Lowe left Gladstone alone on the subject of money until, at the end of 1870, he unveiled his 'currency plan'. Under its provisions the Bank, and all other banks, would cede the power of issuing notes to the Mint, which would extend the £1 note to England with an issue of £15 million. In this way part of the national debt would be monetised, saving an estimated £865,000 of servicing costs per year, without compromising the soundness of money. On the contrary: unsecured private notes would be replaced by a currency secured on the Consolidated Fund, while vesting the power of note issue in the Mint alone would ensure that 'the remedy for a panic would no longer be sought in the debasement of the currency and the deliberate violation of the law in order to attain such debasement'. Furthermore 'we shall explode the mischievous fallacy that creating money is part of the business of banking'.[34]

Lowe pressed his scheme during the winter of 1870–1, repeatedly inquiring of Gladstone how the budget could be balanced *without* some savings on the service of the debt, and even presenting his plan as an eye-catching initiative to freshen up a tired government. 'It is almost impossible to please the public about the War. We want something to strike the public imagination & shew them that our cards are not played out.'[35] Gladstone thought this bad grounds for introducing a reform of which he was in principle 'an ardent supporter', and, far from wanting it as the keystone of the forthcoming budget, sounded the alarm that it might prevent any budget from passing (a role performed in due course by the match tax). 'Your measure brought forward next month would instantly produce a Park Lane jumble and block of business.'[36]

At this, Lowe withdrew his currency plan, returning in 1873 with a very different proposal. The Bank, Lowe now said, should not only keep its power to issue notes but should be able to override the 1844 Bank Charter Act and issue notes unbacked by gold when the Treasury saw fit to declare 'a state of panic'. This they might do 'when the rate of discount at the Bank rises to —— and the exchange has become favourable and great alarm and distrust prevail'. The extra cash, Lowe insisted, 'must be used only for discounting bills of not more than —— days' currency, nor less than —— per cent'. Even so, he had travelled a long way in two years. (Exactly how far would have been revealed only if he had filled in the blanks.)[37]

But this new creed – that the Bank had better have the 1844 rules bent for it than violate them itself – in no way diminished Lowe's conviction that the 1844 Bank Charter Act was one of the greatest achievements of classical political economy. Two days before his 1873 proposal he had responded to a parliamentary motion calling for a Royal Commission to look into and propose remedies for the 'extreme fluctuations in the discount rate as have been frequent since the passing of the Bank Act of 1844'.[38] Lowe told the House how glad he was to hear that it did not wish actually to interfere with the 1844 Act: indeed the current motion 'supported as it had been by such admirable reasoning was not only an intellectual treat, but of real solid advantage to the commercial and free institutions of the country'. The Act had caused neither the fluctuations in the discount rate, which resulted from unavoidable fluctuations in the value of gold, nor the periodic panics, which must continue as long as banks kept inadequate reserves. That, Lowe concluded, was not a matter for the government; it was up to depositors not to put money in these unsafe banks.[39]

11
Beer, Bankruptcy and Empire

Lowe had resigned as a *Times* leader-writer some time before he knew he was to be Chancellor. When he returned to the (opposition) backbenches in 1874, neither he nor Delane suggested a renewal of the role. Instead Lowe became a prolific, brilliant and biting contributor to the political and literary reviews.

Bankruptcy had been an interest of Lowe from his Australian days (see Chapter 1). His post at the Board of Trade had kept him in contact with the issue, his position, as one would expect, being that people should be left to take their own risks. When an MP claimed that discharging bankrupts was unfair to their creditors, Lowe pointed out that creditors lent knowing what the law was and did not have to lend at all. By the time he came to write 'What Shall We Do with Our Bankrupts?' (1881) Lowe had moved on to wanting to abolish the Bankruptcy Court altogether. Creditors could still sue for debt. If they got unequal shares, so what? And if they got nothing, that would teach them to be more careful to whom they lent next time.

As for the debtor, Lowe needed little effort to ridicule the law as it stood in the early 1880s. In the first place, you could be imprisoned for debts of *less* than £50 but not for larger ones. The original reason for this provision had become cloudy, but it was currently being defended as actually helping the poor. If jail were to follow, you would be less likely – and, crucially, seen to be less likely – to default. Therefore credit would be easier to get. Then why stop at jailing debtors, Lowe asked. Why not hang them? Then not only would the debtor exert himself to the utmost but his friends would pay up for him as well. Once creditors saw this, credit would become even easier. This, to Lowe, was reason enough *not* to extend the hangman's clientele. No one should *want* to make it easier for the working class to borrow: 'the curse of the poor is improvidence and intemperance'.[1]

This contrasts with Lowe's earlier defence, *pace* Overstone, of the working man's opportunity to buy shares. Was Lowe thinking of separate strata within the working class? Or was he simply libertarian as long as the poor spent their own money but paternalistic as soon as they started borrowing? Whatever the answer, the 'intemperance' issue urged Lowe on to his other main criticism of the law's anomalies: the fact that you could legally have credit from the baker or the grocer but not from the publican. This, said Lowe, was a fine example of well-intentioned meddling producing the opposite result to the one intended. It simply meant that people borrowed from the grocer and spent the money in the pub, which meant the publican and not the grocer was the one sure of getting his money. 'The legislature' Lowe concluded with triumphant paradox 'has forced on the publican a sound and safe trade'.[2]

The same went for Joseph Chamberlain's eccentric plan to buy up all the public houses in Birmingham in order to close half of them down. Lowe asked if Chamberlain remembered the story of Hoti the swineherd, who burned down his hut in order to roast a single pig. Was he to be taken as the exemplar for this unprecedented forcible suppression of a lawful trade? What about the pubs which, now in municipal hands, were to survive? The Council would have thousands of lucrative places to give away to their own electors. 'Have they no fear that their well meant endeavours to prevent Birmingham becoming a sty of drunkenness may result in turning it into a hotbed of corruption?'[3] Then again, how was the price of council beer to be set? Wherever it ended up, the decision would be politicised with Birmingham at war between 'cheap and dear beer parties',[4] and the consumer would lose as his landlord was replaced by a functionary indifferent to his custom. Above all it was hopelessly naïve to think that reducing the number of pubs would reduce drinking. Who exactly were these people who would stay at home because the walk to the pub was now two minutes longer? They certainly did not include lively men 'qualified to shine' in pub society, or the customer whose wife 'as is so often the case with English women of her class' served up uneatable food, or even anyone who 'just likes drinking'.[5]

As is the case with so many abstemious men, other people's drinking brought out the best in Lowe. Intemperance enabled him to pose the proposition that state interference was ineffective until the working class achieved moral progress and unnecessary once they had done so – a doctrine of which he generally made little compared with the more moralising wing of liberalism. Intemperance, and even bankruptcy, were however minor issues of his alongside the two great (and, to Lowe, intimately linked) questions of Empire and Money.

II

The first thing to be clear about, Lowe wrote in 1877, was that the empire did not make a profit for Britain. Nor had it ever done so. Even the loss of the American colonies had been no loss to the British people financially: they could still emigrate there, settle and prosper, just as before, while the colonists had given Britain negligible help in paying taxes to it, lending to it or fighting for it. Most of the time losing colonies had been a financial gain. The everyday cost of normal administration was considerable, let alone episodes like the one where 'we spent ten millions in order to rescue from captivity three or four British subjects detained in Abyssinia'.[6] Canada and Australia were places Britain was bound to defend but who, if the question of reciprocation ever arose 'will naturally feel regret that they are exposed to loss and injury in a cause which is not theirs'.[7] As for those colonies with the wrong climate for European habitation, their loss would be pure profit.

But Lowe's particular focus in this article was on India. In his *Times* leaders in the 1850s and 1860s he had set out the position that Britain's presence in India, however it had originated, was now an altruistic mission bringing benefits to the Indians and expense to Britain. When, in 1859, 'friends' of India had protested against subjugating it for the first time to income tax, Lowe riposted that those Indians who would be paying it had hitherto enjoyed a European immunity from violence and extortion together with an Asiatic freedom from tax.

> It is for them we have toiled, and ruled, and conquered. Content for ourselves with moderate salaries and reasonable retiring

> allowances, we have enabled them to accumulate enormous wealth, out of which we have never called upon them to contribute one farthing to the public burdens.[8]

But by 1863 Lowe had repented of the modesty of his first encomium.

> We have performed a work mightier than Roman, Assyrian or Macedonian conqueror ever attempted. To conquer and govern vast multitudes of the human race has been their lot, as it has been ours. But to govern them entirely for their own benefit . . . is an honour reserved for England and England alone.[9]

Now, in the 1877 article, he saw the retention of India as bringing not just expense but danger. The acquisition of India might have been by means 'cruel, rapacious and wicked', but the plunderer was now in danger of being plundered 'if not by her, on her behalf. She has become our pet, our darling, our spoilt child.' The 'plunder' was the cost of the 70,000 troops needed to maintain Britain's hold on India. The 'danger' lay in the resulting overstretch of the armed forces. Anyone unable to see that, concluded Lowe, should ask themselves what would have happened had the Mutiny coincided with the Crimean War instead of missing it by a year.[10] As for the writers and orators who represented India as 'the brightest jewel in the British Crown' and held that without it England would sink to a third-rate power, such people were sticking to the opposite of the truth with some exactitude; 'we have in India our greatest, and perhaps our only serious danger'.[11]

So far as he normally found enviable gains for India in any cost incurred by England, Lowe implied that the Raj was an efficient if inequitable operation – more so, he clearly thought, than Britain's government of herself. 'A Simple Way Out of the Indian Difficulty' (1879) is simple at least in its discounting as unthinkable 'the idea that we could under any circumstances deliberately inflict an injury on India for the good of England'.[12]

Lowe's final word on imperialism in general had appeared the previous year. 'Imperialism' (1878) put up a utilitarian standard for assessing the empire – and everything else:

> the one duty of those entrusted with the government of mankind is to act purely and solely, as far as the infirmity of human nature will permit, with the single view of obtaining for that country over which they preside the greatest amount of happiness which the condition of its existence admits of. This is the alpha and omega of the duty of a statesman.[13]

Between the alpha and the omega, however, was the duty not just to practise utilitarianism but to preach it. Otherwise, Lowe very much feared, 'the less informed and more excitable part of the community' would persist in the delusion that 'military glory, success in diplomacy, increase in territory and prestige' were good in themselves, rather than *ad hoc* justifiable on felicific grounds.[14] Especially stubborn was the delusion 'that the happiness of a nation consists in the degree of influence that one people can exercise over the destiny of another'. In fact the conquering nation would never be happy: it could either raise its conquered enemy to a level with itself and so raise discord and sedition too, or hold its people down, in which case 'they will inevitably, as in the case of Rome, drag you down to their own level'.[15] And even Rome had consoled itself in its debasement with the acquisition of slaves, not a modern option. Both ancient and modern experience showed that the way to grow rich was 'not to plunder and ruin other people but to assist them in becoming rich themselves'.[16] To treat others as you would wish to be treated yourself was not just the fairest, but the most 'prudent and judicious' course at imperial as well as personal level. Under Disraeli the Tories had forgotten this. Theirs was an imperialism which actively militated against just imperial rule: by erecting an imperialism which idealised 'the assertion of absolute force over others' they had condemned any scintilla of justice to weigh in as 'so much deducted from its imperial quality'.[17]

In Lowe's final, journalistic phase, two monetary issues dominated – Indian currency and bimetallism. In 1860 he had welcomed India's adoption of the equivalent of the 1844 Act, only with a currency board instead of a central bank. A currency board issuing notes would have political advantages – notes bind people to the existing political system as they realise that if it falls, its banknotes fall with it.[18] But there would also be huge savings from not having to transport gold round India, a point to which Lowe returned when in 1879 he proposed 'A Simple Way Out of the Indian Difficulty'.

The simple way was for India to adopt the gold standard. Indeed, unless she did, her difficulties would get worse. By remaining on a silver standard yet having to pay her share of the cost of imperial administration in gold, she was on the wrong end of an exchange rate which had already deteriorated sharply, and was set to get much worse. 'On this subject', said Lowe, 'it becomes one who has no pretension to the quality of an expert to speak with the utmost moderation and diffidence' – a preamble doubtless discounted by cognisant readers even faster than the Indian silver.[19] In fact Lowe was proposing a gold exchange standard where no gold coins would circulate. By issuing a paper currency fully convertible into gold, the State would raise money for itself without compromising financial stability and, as Lowe had argued in 1860, save the effort and expense of carrying gold around the subcontinent.[20]

The last vestiges of Lowe's moderation and diffidence fled as he raided classical economics for a pedigree for the gold exchange standard. (His appeals to authority generally ended with authority being marched firmly into line.) Mill had contradicted himself on the size of the seignorage gain from issuing notes but only his second position made sense. Ricardo had recommended a gold exchange standard to the 1819 committee of Lords and Commons, but McCulloch had subsequently discredited the proposal by implying, in his *Life and Writings of Ricardo*, that parliament had enacted this but was forced to revert to a straightforward gold standard because it was too easy to forge the banknotes. Not so, said Lowe: the 1819 Act had provided for Ricardo's proposal for two years only. After that it automatically lapsed for reasons which had nothing to do with forgery. Having excluded one reason, Lowe himself lapses into silence about what the true cause was. But with a gold exchange standard, he concludes

> It would be easy without taxing or borrowing to discharge the debt of India and to complete her system of railways. How strange that the treasure should be lying at our feet, and that we will not stoop to pick it up when the alternative is something like national bankruptcy.[21]

While Lowe's enemies had professed to locate a decline in his powers as early as 1871, this vigorous article does not show any sign of it. But in his final contribution to economics, 'What is Money?' (1882) the sarcasm ceases to be a vehicle for economic analysis, and takes over as a substitute. Certainly some of Lowe's victims had not been especially coherent themselves. Explaining whether silver or gold were to be jointly legal tender at a fixed or floating rate was apparently beyond the powers of some of the most distinguished bimetallists. In the end, however, Lowe's own contribution collapses into burlesque:

> I ... must content myself with deploring the unhappy fate of the other metals which, without any fault of their own, are excluded from their right to take part in the metallic congress of which they are also members. In the total absence of any information on the subject, I should have thought that if safety is to be found in numbers, and if two metals are better than one, three must be better than two and four better than three.[22]

Lowe then wraps his argument up by charging that anyone expressing concern about a shortage of gold has neither heard of the specie-flow mechanism nor comprehended that gold 'can be got ... by paying the best price for it'.[23] It was thus perfectly clear that bimetallism 'absolutely destroys the purpose for which money was invented'.[24]

12
Pig Philosophy?

Lowe's definition of political economy was sure and simple. It was the science that traced the consequences of the desire for gain. Its strength lay in the soundness of its basic postulate, and was revealed by the success of laws passed in accordance with the deductions made from that postulate. Particularly impressive was the way that those unable to grasp political economy nonetheless came to believe in it through the results of such laws – though the results might take a while and their clear perception still longer. And, because political economy deduced exact conclusions from first principles, it not only knew when an exception was an exception, but was well placed to find out why. When the world in general, and the results of legislation in particular, diverged from the deductions of political economy, economists sought and invariably found explanations of why *ceteris* had failed to be *paribus*. Falsificationists' problems begin at this point but Lowe, like Mill, was no falsificationist.

Political economy, furthermore, had its own, rather booming, voice – in fact it sounded startlingly like the voice of Robert Lowe. It 'prescribed' freedom of contract, 'forbade' negotiating over tariffs, and 'ruled that' tariffs were only justified in order to collect revenue. Education was 'no exception to the general rules of political economy'. Gladstone's budget of 1860 had 'contaminated the truths of financial science' and the commercial treaty it encompassed had dragged free trade down 'from the dignity of a science to the foggy regions of diplomacy'. Despite such mistakes, most of the laws of the pre-1867 parliament were framed 'in accordance with the principles of political economy', notably the cuts in indirect taxes between 1846 and

1860, and the retention of Irish landlords' freedom to do what they liked with their land.[1]

Some of these statements sound stronger than others. 'In accordance with the laws of political economy' suggests more room for manoeuvre than 'prescribed' or 'ruled' by political economy. But perhaps not too much weight should be placed on this. Lowe was writing leaders in *The Times*, not scholarly articles on the philosophy of science. Probably his exact choice of words was not as exact as all that. What he meant on each occasion was that the principles of political economy could be used to identify what would increase the wealth of the nation, or at least some part of it. (He would have clasped the idea of Pareto-efficiency with enthusiasm had it been around in his time.)

As we indicated in Chapter 6, Lowe was innocent of Mill's charge that some economists had reduced political economy to a series of catchwords. The one catchword he did use regularly was 'political economy' itself. And he did so, as just seen, to point to laws he believed to be both successful and in consonance with its principles. Is this empty sloganising?

Until 1878, Lowe showed little interest in the methodology of economics as such. Like anyone else, he had an implicit methodology of his own. This was determined negatively, by his very limited statement of conditions of application for his economic doctrines. To say that disturbing forces existed but, once identified, they merely reflected back the searchlight of economic analysis in increased splendour, was at once far less sophisticated than Mill's treatment and a superb provocation to the likes of Cliffe Leslie. If Lowe was not especially interested in methodology, the English historical school were not especially interested in anything else. And central to their dispute with Lowe were the roles the two sides had assigned to Adam Smith.

II

Smith, Lowe told the Political Economy Club when it met to celebrate the centenary of *The Wealth of Nations*, was the first and only man to discover a real science of mankind. To discover universal truths about humanity, to weld them into a system of analysis, and then to promulgate that system so that it caught legislators' minds demanded such rare gifts, in such unusual combination, that only one man in history had ever succeeded. In thus placing Ricardo and Mill so firmly in Smith's rearguard, Lowe was also reinforcing what he saw as the methodological unity of the classical school. In his address to Section F of the British Association for the Advancement of Science in 1878, J.K. Ingram followed Cliffe Leslie in driving the stoutest possible wedge between Smith, a historically minded empiricist, and Ricardo, who instead built a mountain of deductions on the unreal stereotype of 'economic man'. In 'Recent Attacks on Political Economy' (1878), Lowe challenged Ingram 'to produce a single instance from *The Wealth of Nations* where Smith has had recourse to the method of induction'.[2] Induction meant inference: Smith observed, compared, explained and illustrated. The one thing he did not do was infer. Division of labour was a good example. First Smith asserted the principle, then he illustrated it. 'Had he proceeded by the inductive method, he would have cited a number of trades in which the division of labour has been found of great advantage and from these instances would have deduced his principle.'[3]

This is not much of a response. Whether actual instances of the division of labour come at the beginning or at the end of Chapter 1 of *The Wealth of Nations* tells us nothing as to how Smith *arrived* at the principle in his mind – as indeed Lowe proceeds to admit: 'Adam Smith . . . professorlike, was more solicitous to teach what he believed to be true than to impart the exact sources from which he derived his information.'[4]

Lowe then compares *The Theory of Moral Sentiments* and *The Wealth of Nations*. Why, asks Lowe, does the former work fail in its leading doctrine that sympathy forms the foundation of morals? (Smith's admirers might well interject at this point that they didn't know it had.) Because *Moral Sentiments* had 'admitted of all motives except the single one of pecuniary interest', with the result that the deductive method 'was not refined enough' for it.[5] In *The Wealth of Nations*, by contrast, Smith isolated the desire for gain, deduced its consequences, compared its predictions with the evidence, and in doing so was entitled to 'the merit, and the unique merit of all men who ever lived in this world, of having founded a deductive and demonstrative science of human conduct'; the 'noble attempt by Bentham and Mill to raise politics to a like eminence' having failed.[6]

Search then the ruling passion; there alone
The wild are constant and the cunning known
The fool consistent, and the false sincere
Priests, princes, women, no dissemblers here.[7]

With Smith boxed up in this fashion, it was an easy step to dismiss historical relativism – though Lowe denied he was doing this. On the contrary, he said, classical economics was itself relativist, insofar as its premises could only be 'brought into existence' by the subject-matter they analysed:

> To suppose that political economists think otherwise is to impute to them a most melancholy economy of brains. All that political economy pretends to is that, when and in proportion as these things come into existence, the principles which apply to them come into existence with them.[8]

Whether this is an ontological point about the 'existence' of ideas, or an empirical claim that men seldom invent theories until their applications are in front of their eyes, it is certainly not relativism as Ingram or Leslie would have understood it. Their relativism was the assertion that you needed different principles to analyse different times and places, each set of principles equally valid in its own context. Lowe in contrast was saying there was a single set of principles which could be applied, once the world had constituted itself into something to apply them to. Until then, there were not alternative varieties of economics: there was no economics.[9] And, when one considers the number of prolegomena to an alternative economics to describe alternative systems (Hodgson [2001] chronicles 150 years of them), who is to say Lowe was wrong? Life, for the historical school, was and is one long inaugural lecture.

III

So the birth of economic science had to wait for a tractable world, and for a genius to perceive that tractable world around him. But, once on its feet, the science had enjoyed huge success, colonising diverse areas of activity in a way which might have surprised its founder. At the *Wealth of Nations* centenary Lowe repeated his 1864 criticism (see Chapter 3) that Smith had not been Smithian enough – though giving him credit for Pitt's French treaty, abolition of monopolies in the colonies and indeed, once the germ of Smith's ideas had been fully worked out by others, the repeal of the Corn Laws and the establishment of limited liability. He also proclaimed himself optimistic that a better educated working class would learn from Smith the 'errors and follies' of trade union behaviour.[10]

The most authentic Lowe thumbprint, however, had been in his 1864 piece – his remark that in other spheres investigation blew up exceptions into alternative rules but in political economy it closed them down. That this, more than anything else, proved the strength and soundness of the subject and its worthiness to be called a science, was a constant refrain of Lowe's. It appears, predictably, in the attack on Ingram, when Lowe asserts that any exceptions to political economy's congruence with experience 'are easily corrected when discovered by the same method of elimination of extraneous motive on which the theory rests', a technique paralleled only on those occasions when mathematics 'directs us . . . sometimes to assume that a very small quantity in comparison with a very large one may be neglected, and that the angles of a polygon, when infinite in number (which is impossible) are equal to a circle'.[11]

Above all political economy was, and would remain, a vastly more successful way of understanding the world than the sociology into which Ingram wanted to subsume it. Back in 1865 Lowe had ridiculed the Social Science Congress for 'professing the cultivation of a branch of human knowledge which as yet has little existence except in its pretentious name'.[12] Now he suggested that Ingram might have accompanied his eulogium of sociology with some evidence that it existed. 'It is a gross abuse of language . . . to degrade the name of science by confounding it with crude and tentative attempts to create science.' Sociology would have been created when it started making verifiable predictions, and when 'the economical phenomena which are treated of in political economy are really dominated by some higher and more comprehensive generalisation'.[13] Expect a long wait, Lowe warned, as long as sociology tried to apply to mankind the inductive method which could only work in the natural scientist's laboratory. Political economy had succeeded precisely because it recognised that human behaviour was so complex as to make a deductive approach not infeasible but unavoidable.

> the facts are often intensely complicated... separated from us often by vast intervals of space and time [and] subject to the distortion, falsification and exaggeration which interest, bigotry, love, hatred, ignorance and party spirit can introduce. We are expected, out of the shreds and fragments of ancient science, life and history which have come down to us mutilated, unvouched and unauthenticated, to recall, with accuracy sufficient for the purposes of science, many things that were utterly hidden from the actors in those remote sciences themselves.[14]

And the measure of its success was what we now owed it:

> among other things, the repeal of hundreds of galling taxes on almost all the comforts of life and on the food of the people, the repeal of the corn and navigation laws, the cessation of smuggling, the placing of the currency on a thoroughly sound and satisfactory basis, the establishment of limited liability in joint-stock companies, the principle of payment by results, open competition for public appointments, and the abolition of the absurd system of bounties and drawbacks. These are some of the achievements of the past. I may be excused if I prefer them to the shadowy and unrealised anticipations of the future.[15]

Lowe's article drew a swift response from Cliffe Leslie. Its theme was that orthodox economists who looked at Lowe would see only a mildly distorted version of their own basic principles – distorted, indeed, by an honesty which they themselves lacked. Certainly Lowe had exposed the absurdity of his own views, said Leslie, offering up targets like the remark that 'if you place a man's ear within the ring of pounds, shillings and pence, his conduct can be counted on to the greatest nicety'.[16] But there was no great distinction between Lowe's omission of all human motives except the desire for wealth, and the fate of these motives in the work of Mill and Cairnes, where they were 'admitted at the outset for form's sake, to be afterwards set aside as "disturbing causes" in a manner without precedent or analogy in physical science'.[17]

However, in the matter of prediction in economics, Leslie did drive a qualitative wedge between Lowe and Mill or Cairnes. Lowe failed to realise, Leslie said, that his simplistic assumptions and his goal of prediction were incompatible: by throwing out so many motives he had no hope of success in the prediction he valued so highly. At least Mill had realised that conclusions derived from the *a priori* method were 'true only in the abstract' and would be 'true without qualification only in purely imaginary cases'.[18]

This limitation came about precisely because Mill had effectively removed so many human motives from the cognisance of political economy. And this situation would continue as long as economists clung to Cairnes' doctrine that 'the economist starts with a knowledge of ultimate causes [and] is already at the outset of his enterprise, in the position which the physicist only attains after ages of laborious research'.[19] On that basis, the foundation of all economics must be introspection and so – unless deductivists imagined that they could also intuit all moral, religious, political and other motives influencing human conduct – they were stuck with a 'science' effectively just as narrow as Lowe's version.

Leslie saw nothing wrong with prediction as one of the goals of economics, and indeed went out of his way to stress the power of prediction if the agenda were only widened. It was because marriages and births were the result of 'love, chivalrous sentiment, morals and religion' that their incidence could be foretold.[20] But on the whole it was failure to understand, not failure to predict, which he condemned as the inevitable result of the method recommended by Lowe. Look at the German economy, so geared towards war. What would be the worth of a treatise deducing its characteristics 'from the assumption that every man is occupied solely in the acquisition of wealth'?[21] Lowe (and by implication Mill and Cairnes) had ruled himself out from explaining why economies differed in their basic structure, occupational patterns and consumers' wants.[22]

Lowe no doubt took the final charge with equanimity. He had already invited economists to share his indifference as to whether people preferred to grow pigs or tulips. But Leslie also charged that Lowe's methodology stopped him having anything to say about why some economies grew while others stagnated. Enough has been said for the reader to imagine the depth of Lowe's indignation on this score. His entire defence of classical political economy rested on the idea that without its doctrines there would have been no liberal legislation and without liberal legislation Britain would be much less prosperous. Nor does Leslie disagree with this: his accusation is rather that Lowe has misunderstood the character of classical (or at any rate Smithian) economics.

> Mr Lowe arrogates 'triumphs' for his own economic method: those he refers to were achieved by the opposite method of reasoning from observation and experience.[23]

Leslie could hardly have made himself clearer. Political economy could indeed claim legislative triumphs which had fostered the general good, and he and Lowe could agree what those triumphs were, whatever their differences about the underlying nature of the political economy which had produced them. It was left for Moore (1996) to adjudicate that Lowe had made mercantile success the only criterion of the success of political economy and thus justified Carlyle's jibe about 'pig philosophy'.[24] On the basis of the remark quoted above, Leslie ought to join Lowe in the trough.

But Lowe was not a pig philosopher. He was an idiosyncratic, but not profoundly original, classical survivor who, like most of his contemporaries, saw nothing wrong with evaluating economics by the results of legislation passed in consonance with its principles. He would not go down well at a modern conference on the methodology of economics, but neither would a great many other people whose porcine qualities are not obviously to the fore.

13
Vapulo, Veneo, Exulo, Fio

Like most people, Lowe dated his old age from his entry to the House of Lords. It was an institution to which he had always been indulgent. Even when, after 1874, he complained that its Tory majority removed the last restraint on Beaconsfieldism, he blamed not so much the Lords for permitting the outrage as Disraeli for taking advantage of it.

But making excuses for the Lords made him no more willing to go there himself. On becoming Viscount Sherbrooke in 1880, he told a correspondent that, with no offer of a place in Gladstone's new government, he 'had no choice but to take [a peerage] though it was the last thing I wanted. My position is best described by the three [*sic*] neuter verbs in the Latin Grammar

> Vapulo, I am beaten
> Veneo I am sold
> Exulo I am banished
> Fio I am done'.[1]

And, to the same correspondent a year later:

> Now I am like Giant Despair in Pilgrim's Progress who can only grin at the people whom he once would have eaten.[2]

Opportunities for retired politicians to intrude themselves were fewer then than now. But in any case Lowe's physical and mental decline, accelerating after 1885, would have kept him more or less out of public life. With total blindness catching up with him at last, and failing memory, no one has claimed that his last years were happy ones, consoled though they were by foreign travels with his loving and much younger second wife. His last political act was to attend a meeting of Liberal Unionists after the Home Rule split of 1886. Martin (1893) barely refers to this; no subsequent biography mentions it at all. This is hardly a major omission – little was made of the incident at the time by Liberals, or Unionists, or Lowe himself. There is no indication that he might have eventually followed his confreres into the Conservative party, and in any case his active political life was now over.

James Bryce's study of Lowe, published in 1903, 11 years after Lowe's death, asked if any other case could be found of so steep a descent from fame to oblivion while still alive. Had Lowe been as thoroughly forgotten as Bryce makes out? It sounds unlikely, but no one will be sure now.

II

Lowe scorned sociology, or what passed for it in his lifetime, but his deepest convictions – taking precedence over even his economic liberalism – may properly be called sociological. There are two ways to get an economic liberal to talk about class. One is to put him in a society full of legal privileges for sectional interests. The other is to confront him with collectivist views themselves dominated by class. The second method barely worked on Lowe. He was enthusiastic enough in his search for intellectual positions to attack. They did not include socialism or communism, which he *did* use simply as catch-phrases (again wrong-footing Mill and his list). It was John Morley, not Lowe, who apprised Gladstone of the very interesting ideas of Dr Marx of Highgate.

But class privilege was a lifelong target. 'The ideal of the Liberal Party' he said in 1878

> consists in a view of things undisturbed and undistorted by the promptings of interest and prejudice, in a complete independence of all class interests, and in relying for its success on the better feelings of mankind.[3]

Hence his revealing statement that 'the grand principle of Free Trade... that no one class in the country should be made tributary to another class' was far more valuable than free trade itself. Hence his anger when Overstone tried to exclude the poor from shareholding and his insistence – more intense and protracted than any of his contemporaries – that the tax system be fair to all classes. Hence, even, by Lowe's own lights, his speeches on the franchise.

Yet some of Lowe's treatment of class issues delineates the limits on his liberalism. The much quoted passage where he called for education which would keep the lower classes 'deferring to higher cultivation when they meet it' must, despite Sylvester's (1974) efforts in Lowe's defence, be taken at face value. It is significant, though, that it is the cultural ingredients for good government that Lowe is considering here. He may have been a 'meritocrat' even in the political sphere, but here 'merit' began where the necessities of a degree and gentlemanly manners left off. Statecraft might include work 'too dirty for aristocratic hands', as Lowe commented of his vice-presidency of the Education Board, but, in Professor Winter's words, Lowe never confused statecraft with entrepreneurship. Efficiency might be a watchword in political as in economic life, but a larger efficiency required that, though social ladders be available, they should not be so available as to unsettle the majority who would always fail to climb them.

When Lowe stopped looking downwards and looked upwards, such reservations ceased. Here equity and efficiency fell into line. Lowe's dislike of deference towards the upper class (as opposed to deference to the intellectual qualities too few of them possessed) sat easily with his objection to privileges for the already wealthy. His distaste for heraldry and armorial bearings is significant – mere boredom would mean nothing. More directly economic was his rebuke to the rich archaeologists who wanted him to channel them taxes paid by the working man to support their hobby. But in his most remarkable onslaught on deference, unsurprisingly omitted when he published his *Poems of a Life* (1885), he aimed at the highest target he could find.

In 1875 the royal yacht, with Victoria on board, was crossing the Solent when it ploughed into a small schooner, killing three of its crew. None of the royal party was hurt, but much of the press begged the Queen to accept their deep sympathy in the shock she had undergone. This was too much for the former Chancellor of the Exchequer:

> Oh weep for the living and not for the dead
> Oh weep for the noble and not for the mean
> We cannot deny that three spirits are fled
> But then only think how they frightened the Queen
>
> If Majesty please to drive straight through the water
> As swift as the lightning that spares not nor swerves
> It is not enough to submit to the slaughter
> We ought to submit without shaking her nerves
>
> Disloyal and selfish they might have contrived it
> The wreck of their being from notice to screen
> They died and their victim thank heaven survived it
> But then only think how they frightened the Queen.[4]

It would be unfair to much of the nineteenth-century Conservative party to identify it with the kind of sycophancy lambasted in these lines. It is unlikely, however, that any Conservative politician would have been able or desirous to write them and, without wanting to load too much portentousness on some savagely comic light verse, they do reinforce the point that Lowe could never have been at home outside the Liberal party.

Or not until 1979, in his 168th year. And when economic liberalism did come back into fashion, in the Tory party and more generally, he did not feature among the forgotten libertarian sages now rewarded with disinterment. No one founded a Sherbrooke Society or presented Mrs Thatcher with a Robert Lowe tie. Yet his crusade to free society from statism and vested interests, his recognition that these two enemies were intimately linked, make him an apt enough man-of-the-times for the last two decades of the twentieth century.

There will always be those who say that the removal of sectional privileges itself privileges the class that alone does not have to rely on such assistance to begin with – the ruling class, or the owners of the means of production, if one wants to put it in Marxist language. There is much to be said for this view but Lowe would not have said it. In the end he would have probably been happy with, and felt he had earned, an epitaph that he fought for justice. In fact his memorial received some rather plodding Latin, composed by Lord Selborne, about putting country before party.

But of course Lowe never saw this. Instead he enjoyed, shared around, and even had Gladstone translate into Italian and Greek, some lines sent him anonymously at the end of his Chancellorship.

> Here lie the bones of Robert Lowe
> Where he's gone I do not know
> If to the realms of peace and love
> Farewell to happiness above;
> If to a place of lower level
> I can't congratulate the Devil.

Biographical Notes

Arnold, Matthew (1822–88). Educ. Winchester and Balliol College, Oxford. Chief HM. Inspector of Schools; poet and author of *Culture and Anarchy* (1869).

Ayrton, Acton Smee (1816–86). Liberal MP 1857–74. Parliamentary Secretary to the Treasury 1868–9; First Commissioner of Works 1869–73; Judge-advocate-general 1873–4.

Bagehot, Walter (1826–77). Educ. Bristol College and University College, London. Editor, *The Economist*, 1860–77.

Bright, John (1811–89). Educ. four different schools. Liberal MP 1843–89; President of the Board of Trade 1868–70; Chancellor of the Duchy of Lancaster 1873–4, 1880–2.

Cairnes, John Elliott (1823–75). Educ. Trinity College, Dublin. Whately Professor of Political Economy, Trinity College, Dublin 1856–61; Professor of Political Economy and Jurisprudence, University College, Galway 1859–65; Professor of Political Economy, University College, London 1866–75.

Cardwell, Edward (1813–86). Educ. Winchester and Balliol College, Oxford. Conservative MP 1842–6; Peelite and Liberal MP 1847–74; President of the Board of Trade 1852–5; Secretary for Ireland 1859–61; Secretary for the Colonies 1864–6; Secretary for War 1868–74; Viscount Cardwell from 1874.

Clarendon, Earl of (George William Frederick Villiers, 1800–70). Educ. St John's College, Cambridge. Lord Privy Seal 1839–41; Chancellor of the Duchy of Lancaster 1840–1; Lord Lieutenant of Ireland 1847–52; Foreign Secretary 1853–8, 1865–6, 1868–70; Chancellor of the Duchy of Lancaster 1864–5.

Cobden, Richard (1804–65). Educ. at prototype of Dotheboys Hall. Liberal MP 1841–65; Leader of the Anti-Corn Laws campaign.

Cross, Richard Assheton (1823–1914). Educ. Rugby and Trinity College, Cambridge. Conservative MP 1857–62, 1868–86; Home Secretary 1874–80, 1885–6; Secretary for India 1886–92; Lord Privy Seal 1895–1900; Viscount Cross from 1886.

Delane, John Thaddeus (1817–79). Educ. private schools, King's College, London and Magdalen College, Oxford. Editor of *The Times*, 1841–77.

Dilke, Sir Charles Wentworth (1843–1911). Educ. privately and at Trinity Hall, Cambridge. Liberal MP 1868–86, 1892–1911; Under-Secretary, Foreign Office 1880–2; President of Local Government Board 1882–5.

Disraeli, Benjamin (1804–81). Educ. privately. Conservative MP 1837–76; Leader of the House of Commons and Chancellor of the Exchequer 1852, 1858–9, 1866–8; Prime Minister 1868, 1874–80; Earl of Beaconsfield from 1876.

Fawcett, Henry (1833–84). Educ. K.C.S. London, Peterhouse and Trinity Hall, Cambridge. Seventh Wrangler 1856. Fellow of Trinity Hall 1856–84; Professor of Political Economy, Cambridge 1863–84; Liberal MP 1865–84; Postmaster-General 1880–4.

Fortescue, Chichester Samuel (1823–98). Educ. privately and at Christ Church, Oxford. Liberal MP 1847–74; Chief Secretary for Ireland 1865–6, 1868–70; President of the Board of Trade 1871–4; Lord Privy Seal 1881–5; Lord President of the Council 1883–5; Lord Carlingford from 1874.

Gipps, Sir George (1791–1847). Educ. King's School, Canterbury and the Military Academy, Woolwich. Governor of New South Wales 1838–46.

Gladstone, William Ewart (1809–98). Educ. Eton and Christ Church, Oxford. Conservative MP 1832–46, Peelite 1847–59, Liberal 1859–95; President of the Board of Trade 1843–5; Colonial Secretary 1845–6; Chancellor of the Exchequer 1852–5, 1859–66, 1873–4, 1880–2; Prime Minister 1868–74, 1880–5, 1886, 1892–4.

Goschen, George Joachim (1831–1907). Educ. Rugby and Oriel College Oxford. Liberal MP 1863–86; Conservative MP 1887–1900. First Lord of the Admiralty 1871–4, 1895–1900; Chancellor of the Exchequer 1887–92; Viscount Goschen from 1900.

Hubbard, John Gellibrand (1805–89). Educ. privately and in Bordeaux. Governor of the Bank of England 1853–5; Conservative MP 1859–68, 1874–7; Lord Addington from 1887.

Hunt, George Ward (1825–77). Educ. Eton and Christ Church, Oxford. Conservative MP 1857–77; Chancellor of the Exchequer 1868; First Lord of the Admiralty 1874–7.

Ingram, John Kells (1823–1907). Educ. Newry Scholl and Trinity College, Dublin. Fellow of Trinity College, Dublin 1846; Professor of Oratory and English Literature 1852; Regius Professor of Greek 1866.

Jevons, William Stanley (1835–82). Educ. University College School and University College, London. Assayer to the mint of Sydney, Australia 1854–9; Professor of Logic and of Political, Mental and Moral Philosophy, Owens College, Manchester 1866–80; Author of *Theory of Political Economy* (1871).

Leslie, Thomas Edward Cliffe (1827–82). Educ. King William's College, I.O.M. and Trinity College, Dublin. Professor of Jurisprudence and political economy, Queen's College, Belfast 1853–82.

Lewis, Sir George Cornewall (1806–63). Educ. Eton and Christ Church. Liberal MP 1847–52, 1855–63; Financial Secretary to the Treasury 1850–2; Editor, *Edinburgh Review* 1852–5; Chancellor of the Exchequer 1855–8; Home Secretary 1859–61; Secretary for War 1861–3.

Lingen, Sir Ralph Robert Wheeler (1819–1905). Educ. Bridgnorth School and Trinity College, Oxford. Secretary to Committee of Council on Education 1849–69; Permanent Secretary at the Treasury 1869–85; Lord Lingen from 1885.

McCulloch, John Ramsay (1789–1864). Educ. at Kinross and at Edinburgh University. Professor of Political Economy, University College, London 1828–32; Comptroller, Her Majesty's Stationery Office 1838–64; Author of *Principles of Political Economy* (1825), *Principles of Taxation* (1845).

Mill, John Stuart (1806–73). Educ. by his father. Author of *A System of Logic* (1843), *Principles of Political Economy* (1848), *On Liberty* (1859), *Utilitarianism* (1863); Liberal MP 1865–8.

Morley, John (1838–1923). Educ. Cheltenham and Lincoln College, Oxford. Liberal MP 1883–1908; Chief Secretary for Ireland 1886, 1892–5; Secretary of State for India 1905–10; Lord Privy Seal 1910–14; Viscount Morley from 1908.

Overstone, Lord (Samuel Jones Loyd, 1796–1883). Educ. Eton and Trinity College, Cambridge. Banker; chairman of Irish Famine Committee 1847; Author of *Reflections on the State of the Currency* (1837).

Palmerston, Viscount (Henry John Temple, 1784–1865). Educ. Harrow and St John's College, Cambridge. Tory MP 1807–28; Whig/Liberal MP 1828–65; Foreign Secretary 1830–4, 1835–41, 1846–51; Home Secretary 1852–5; Prime Minister 1855–8, 1859–65.

Senior, Nassau William (1790–1864). Educ. Eton and Magdalen College, Oxford. Drummond Professor of Political Economy, Oxford 1825–30, 1847–52; Author of *Outline of the Science of Political Economy* (1836).

Smith, William Henry (1825–91). Conservative MP 1868–91. First Lord of the Admiralty 1877–80; Secretary for War 1885, 1886; Leader of the House 1886–91.

Torrens, Colonel Robert (1780–1864). Army officer; proprietor of *Globe* newspaper; Whig MP 1831–5. Author of *An Essay on Money and Paper Currency* (1812), *Essay on the External Corn Trade* (1815).

Wilson, James (1805–60). Educ. Quaker schools. Founder (1843) and first editor of *The Economist*. Liberal MP 1847–59; Financial Secretary to the Treasury 1853–8; Vice-President of the Board of Trade 1858–9; the financial member of the Council of India 1859–60.

Notes

1 Go out and govern New South Wales

1. Robert Lowe, 'Success' (1869), quoted in Arthur Patchett Martin, *Life and Letters of the Right Honourable Robert Lowe, Viscount Sherbrooke*, London, 1893, vol. 2, p. 359.
2. Ibid., vol. 2, p. 358.
3. Though Charles Wood's budget of 1851 fell with Lord John Russell's government, and contained substantial revisions on its eventual reintroduction after the government's reappointment.
4. Martin, *Life and Letters*, vol. 1, p. 43.
5. Ibid., vol. 1, p. 43.
6. Ibid., vol. 2, pp. 393–4.
7. Ibid., vol. 1, p. 84.
8. James Winter, *Robert Lowe*, Toronto, 1976.
9. Gillian Knight, *Illiberal Liberal: Robert Lowe in New South Wales, 1842–1850*, Melbourne, 1966, p. 119.
10. Winter, *Robert Lowe*, p. 45.
11. Martin, *Life and Letters*, vol. 1, p. 329. This was in line with the theory of colonisation advanced by Edward Gibbon Wakefield, a doctrine much praised by J.S. Mill as identifying a case of market failure and an appropriate remedy by the state (J.S. Mill, *Principles of Political Economy*, variorum edition in J.M. Robson (ed.), *The Collected Works of John Stuart Mill*, Toronto, 1967, vol. 3, pp. 958–9, 963–6).
12. Martin, *Life and Letters*, vol. 1, p. 330.
13. Knight, *Illiberal Liberal*, p. 182.
14. Speech by Robert Lowe, 27 July 1848, quoted in Knight, *Illiberal Liberal*, p. 202.
15. Knight, *Illiberal Liberal*, p. 216.
16. Martin, *Life and Letters*, vol. 1, p. 371.
17. Ibid., p. 372.
18. Knight, *Illiberal Liberal*, p. 61. It was not just the suffering of the imprisoned debtors, he said. The threat of prison led to 'fire-sale' liquidations which further enriched landowners at the expense of the poor.
19. Ibid., p. 63.
20. Report, *Sydney Morning Herald*, 5 July 1848, quoted in Knight, *Illiberal Liberal*, p. 194.

2 The limits to *laissez-faire*

1. *The Times*, 26 February 1851, p. 4.
2. *Hansard*, 3rd series, 126, 935, 2 May 1853.
3. *Hansard*, 145, 1162–3, 4 June 1857.
4. *Hansard*, 140, 124, 1 February 1856.
5. *Hansard*, 140, 127, 1 February 1856.
6. *Hansard*, 140, 138, 1 February 1856.
7. To be exact, the bill would have ensured that a lender who took his return in the form of a share of the firm's profits would be treated as favourably as any other creditor if the firm went bankrupt. Some MPs, but not Lowe, classified this arrangement as a form of partnership.
8. *The Times*, 11 June 1866, p. 8.
9. *The Times*, 11 June 1866, p. 8.
10. *Parliamentary Papers*, 1857–8, vol. 14, Select Committee on Accidents on Railways, pp. 620–4.
11. *The Times*, 11 September 1858, p. 6.
12. James Winter, *Robert Lowe*, p. 153.
13. Ibid., p. 155.

3 Trade and treaties

1. For the limits on the role of *any* political economy in the Repeal debate, see A. Boyd Hilton, *The Age of Atonement* (CUP, 1988).
2. Mill did not publish the theory until 1844. See 'On the Laws of Interchange Between Nations' (1844) reprinted in J.M. Robson (ed.), *The Collected Works of John Stuart Mill*, Toronto, 1967, vol. 4, pp. 232–61.
3. Mill thought 'considerations of reciprocity' might be taken into account when a tariff was there, or was planned, in order to raise revenue. Was Mill being logical? As no one disagreed with tariffs in order to raise revenue in the first place, reciprocity would seem irrelevant. Perhaps Mill meant it should be used to choose between two alternative tariffs equally effective at raising revenue. See Douglas A. Irwin, *Against the Tide: An Intellectual History of Free Trade*, Princeton, NJ, 1996, p. 109.
4. Palmerston to Cowley, 30 January 1860, quoted in E.D. Steele, *Palmerston and Liberalism*, Cambridge, 1991, p. 97.
5. Gladstone to Lacaita, 1 December 1860, quoted in A. Howe, *Free Trade and Liberal England, 1846–1946*, Oxford, 1997, p. 173.
6. *Hansard*, 157, 314, 9 March 1860. However, even if Gladstone had been right in strictly economic terms, France had won an acceptance of her annexation of Nice and Savoy that Britain 'would not have given so readily without a reduction in the French tariff' (Peter Marsh, *Bargaining on Europe: Britain and the First Common Market, 1860–1892*, Yale, 1999, p. 12).
7. *Hansard*, 156, 835, 10 February 1860. A.L. Dunham's study of 1930, still the most comprehensive account of the treaty, unkindly accuses Gladstone of confusing brandy with wine, it being the latter which, unwillingly, he

had to let in cheap or see the treaty wrecked (Dunham, *The Anglo-French Treaty of Commerce of 1860*, Norwood, pp. 89–90).

8. As the French themselves appreciated: 'I believe that the good sense of the House of Commons would never have carried the day in this stormy debate without the conspicuous ability of the Chancellor of the Exchequer', the French ambassador reported back to his foreign minister (Dunham, *The Anglo-French Treaty of Commerce*, p. 117).
9. Steele, *Palmerston and Liberalism*, p. 97.
10. A. Howe, *Free Trade and Liberal England*, Oxford, 1997, p. 94.
11. *History of the Times*, London, 1936–9, vol. 2, pp. 131ff. There is only one instance in the letters of Delane telling Lowe what to write: Delane wanted an editorial on some negotiations taking place with Canada and urged Lowe not to 'throw too much cold water upon it'. Lowe complied with the first part of the request, but refused the second. Where Lowe's own feelings were not engaged he was willing to be a 'passive instrument'; and on another occasion he checked that Delane's view concurred with his own before writing anything. As for editorial alteration of Lowe's leaders after he sent them in, there is one instance of Lowe approving a piece of editing as actually amplifying his own view, and one of Lowe regretfully informing Delane that no change could be made as the leader was already in the press. On the other side of the coin, Lowe was more than willing to tell Delane what to write, notably in 1863 when Delane had got drawn into a long-running row between Cobden and Lowe. Later Delane received a severe rebuke for being insufficiently hostile to the Second Reform Bill. The friendship between the two men was close (it was in Delane that Lowe chose to confide the details of his deteriorating marriage) but the correspondence reads as if neither forgot that Delane had once been Lowe's pupil at Oxford. Delane Papers, News International, JTD 12/136 (21 and 23 December 1863), JTD 14/16 (12 and 13 June 1865), JTD 15/6 (10 January 1866), JTD 15/41 (28 March 1866), JTD 15/62 (28 June 1866), JTD 16/12 (22 January 1867), JTD 14/109 (15 December 1865).
12. *The Times*, 16 January 1860, p. 6.
13. *The Times*, 23 January 1860, p. 6.
14. 'Commercial Diplomacy, 1860–1902', printed for private circulation by the Foreign Office, 1902. PRO T 172/945, p. 5.
15. This is not to dismiss the British businessmens' contribution as insignificant. The Bradford Chamber of Commerce were particularly effective. In Peter Marsh's words 'their concrete criticisms . . . finally wore the French down' so that most textiles ended up with a much lower duty than France had first proposed (*Bargaining on Europe*, p. 17f.). Moreover such deputations were there at the enthusiastic invitation of the French government, to rebut French protectionist manufacturers whom the French minister of commerce believed had 'lied wholesale to the Emperor and the members of the Commission' (Cobden's diary, 26 April 1860, quoted in Dunham, *The Anglo-French Treaty of Commerce*, p. 127).

16. 'The vision of protectionist propaganda throughout France, with deputations besieging the government offices in Paris, was most unpleasant to contemplate' (Dunham, *The Anglo-French Treaty of Commerce*, p. 75).
17. *The Times*, 7 May 1860, p. 8.
18. *The Times*, 1 August 1860, p. 8.
19. *The Times*, 4 December 1860, p. 8.
20. *The Times*, 27 May 1862, pp. 9–10.
21. *The Times*, 19 February 1863, p. 8.
22. *The Times*, 15 April 1861, p. 8.
23. *The Times*, 17 January 1865, p. 6. It was Lowe's *Times* leaders that made the repeated, and inaccurate, assertion that 'protection was as much a cause of the disruption of the Union as slavery'. *The Times*, 12 March 1861, p. 9.
24. *The Times*, 15 April 1861, p. 8.
25. *The Times*, 27 May 1862, p. 10.
26. *The Times*, 19 February 1863, p. 8.
27. An editorial by Lowe, 30 August 1861, had said that when 'the prosperity of the country and the subsistence of millions' was at stake, the government, as well as the Manchester Cotton Company, should go out to India and Egypt and 'strain every nerve' to develop alternative supplies of cotton. The State and the company were already building, and must continue to build, roads, docks and factories.
28. *The Times*, 6 July 1863, p. 8.
29. *Hansard*, 3rd series, 177, 1861, 17 March 1865.
30. *Hansard*, 177, 1863, 17 March 1865. Disraeli had made the same point as early as 1863: 'You have played all your cards' (*Hansard*, 169, 442–3, 17 March 1863). The recent study by Peter Marsh agrees: 'The example that Britain set in scuttling most of its tariff found few continental admirers and all but destroyed Britain's bargaining power' (*Bargaining on Europe*, p. 52).
31. *The Times*, 20 August 1861, p. 10.
32. *The Times*, 30 January 1864, p. 8.
33. *Hansard*, 181, 609–10, 16 February 1866.
34. *Hansard*, 181, 618, 16 February 1866.
35. *Hansard*, 181, 621, 16 February 1866.
36. *The Times*, 11 August 1865, p. 6.
37. *The Times*, 23 November 1865, p. 8.
38. *Hansard*, 201, 163–6, 3 May 1870.
39. Lowe to Gladstone, Gladstone Papers, 1870 [n.d.] British Library, Add. Mss. 44310, ff. 58–9. He also took the chance to reassert his unilateralist principles, telling a delegation from the Associated Chambers of Commerce that 'if they were to negotiate with Spain and Portugal, they would in effect be conferring an immense advantage upon them for their illiberality' (Marsh, *Bargaining on Europe*, p. 74).
40. Lowe, unlike some Liberals, never made much of the idea that tariff reductions were desirable insofar as they cut off a source of revenue and

thus forced governments to be economical (see Howe, *Free Trade and Liberal England*, pp. 113f.).

41. For an excellent account of Lowe's position on the issue as Chancellor, see A. Iliasu, *The Role of Free Trade Treaties in British Foreign Policy, 1859–1871*, Ph.D. thesis, University of London, 1965, Chapter 7.
42. And told Bright (27 December 1869) he had come to 'loathe' the haggling of commercial diplomacy (Marsh, *Bargaining on Europe*, p. 71). Lowe's stand on the issue, at the very least, can have done him no harm when Gladstone was looking around for a Chancellor in 1868.
43. F.O. 146/1615, 9 October 1871. See also Iliasu, *Role of Free Trade Treaties*, pp. 404–6.
44. See Howe, *Free Trade and Liberal England*, p. 160.
45. Lowe to Gladstone, 7 October 1872, Gladstone Papers, British Library, Add. Mss. 44302, f. 92.
46. R. Lowe, 'Reciprocity and Free Trade', *Nineteenth Century*, vol. 5, June 1878, p. 995.
47. Ibid., p. 1002.
48. *The Times*, 14 October 1858, p. 6.
49. *The Times*, 27 September 1861, p. 6.
50. *The Times*, 3 March 1860, p. 8.
51. R. Lowe, 'A New Reform Bill', *Fortnightly Review*, 22, 1 October 1877, p. 449.
52. See *The Times*, 27 February 1860, p. 8 and 1 August 1860, p. 8.
53. *The Times*, 24 November 1860, p. 8.
54. *The Times*, 25 March 1861, p. 8.
55. *The Times*, 9 June 1864, p. 10.
56. *The Times*, 22 August 1862, p. 6.
57. R. Lowe, 'The Past Session and the New Parliament', *Edinburgh Review*, 105, April 1857, p. 553.
58. Ibid., p. 554. Party lines, in both senses of the phrase, were still much less rigidly set than they were to become; to generalise about a party's intake in a particular election was itself rather progressive.
59. Ibid., p. 571.
60. R. Lowe, Preface to *Speeches and Letters on Reform*, London, John Robert Bush, 1867, pp. 3–4.
61. Ibid., pp. 4–5.

4 Education, education, administration

1. Lowe to Sir John Simon, 31 October 1868, quoted in D.W. Sylvester, *Robert Lowe on Education*, Cambridge, 1974, p. 23.
2. E.G. West, 'Public versus Private Education', *Journal of Political Economy*, 72, October 1964, reprinted in A.W. Coats (ed.), *The Classical Economists and Economic Policy*, London, 1971, p. 141.
3. R. Lowe, *Middle Class and Primary Education*, Liverpool, 1868, pp. 7–8.
4. Ibid., p. 9.

5. *The Times*, 22 March 1869, p. 6.
6. These attitudes might have led Mill to call for a general system of State education. But universal State education, he wrote in *On Liberty*, 'is a mere contrivance for moulding people to be exactly like each other... An education established and controlled by the State should only exist, if it exists at all, as one among many competing experiments, carried on for the purpose of example and stimulus, to keep others up to a certain standard of excellence'. Mill, *On Liberty*, quoted by Mark Blaug in A. Skinner and T. Wilson (eds), *Essays on Adam Smith*, Oxford, 1975, p. 585.
7. *Middle Class and Primary Education*, p. 12.
8. Speech at London University, 3 February 1874, reported in *The Times*, 4 February 1874, p. 5.
9. West, 'Public versus Private Education', p. 141.
10. *Hansard*, 3rd series, 165, 229, 13 February 1862.
11. Lowe to Ralph Lingen, 13 February 1881, quoted Arthur Patchett Martin, *Life and Letters of the Right Honourable Robert Lowe, Viscount Sherbrooke*, London, 1893, vol. 2, p. 217.
12. *Hansard*, 164, 729, 11 July 1861.
13. The only remaining safeguard was that if a schoolmaster placed *all* his children in the lowest or second lowest grade, there would be a deduction on this evidence that the instruction 'was not what it ought to be', *Hansard*, 176, 552, 30 June 1864.
14. James Winter, *Robert Lowe*, Toronto, 1976, p. 186.
15. *Hansard*, 166, 1239–43, 5 May 1862.
16. Winter, *Robert Lowe*, p. 186.
17. *Hansard*, 188, 1548–9, 15 July 1867.
18. Speech at Edinburgh, 1 November 1867, reported in *The Times*, 4 November 1867, p. 8.
19. *The Times*, 4 November 1867, p. 8. He had already discouraged hopes that the workers would pick up enough political economy to cease 'depriv[ing] themselves of wages at the bidding of the worst among them', citing Smith's cultural pessimism about the effects of division of labour in order to rule out the labourers learning much from Smith. *The Times*, 12 November 1859, p. 8.
20. Lowe, *Primary and Classical Education* (an expanded version of his Edinburgh speech), Edinburgh, 1867, p. 32.
21. Speech, 22 January 1868, at annual dinner of Liverpool Philomathic Society, reported in *The Times*, 24 January 1868, p. 5.
22. *The Times*, 24 January 1868, p. 5.
23. Ibid.
24. *The Times*, 17 September 1872, p. 6.
25. Lord George Hamilton, *Parliamentary Reminiscences and Reflections, 1868–85*, London, 1916, pp. 157–8.
26. *The Times*, 24 January 1868, p. 5.
27. Elementary education became compulsory in 1881; most schools became completely free in 1891.
28. *The Times*, 6 December 1871, p. 3.

29. *The Times*, 1 February 1879, p. 8.
30. *The Times*, 2 November 1867, p. 8.
31. *The Times*, 18 November 1868, p. 6.
32. *The Times*, 6 December 1871, p. 3.
33. *Hansard*, 214, 1483–4, 6 March 1873. Lowe, with Gladstone's support, succeeded in separating the teaching and examination functions in the Irish Universities Bill of 1873, though his cabinet colleague the Duke of Argyll and Scottish Universities MP Lyon Playfair opposed the separation on the grounds that education would be displaced by cramming. Lowe was killing two birds with one stone: the Act removed part of Trinity College, Dublin's endowment to pay for the examining board. See Jonathan Parry, *Democracy and Religion: Gladstone and the Liberal Party 1867–1885*, Cambridge, 1986, pp. 135, 353–4.
34. Martin, *Life and Letters*, vol. 2, p. 363.
35. *The Times*, 26 February 1877, p. 8 and 27 February 1877, p. 8. Lowe's reaction was to move on to the 'monstrous abuse that the Universities should teach only half the year', an abuse which prevented the introduction of two-year degrees. *Hansard*, 234, 134, 30 April 1877.
36. R. Lowe, 'Shall We Create a New University?', *Fortnightly Review*, 21, new series, 1 December 1877, pp. 160–71.
37. Lowe failed to revive his 1858 suggestion that the Civil Service Commission should not only choose messenger boys on their academic performance but should move into the universities and examine degrees directly. *Hansard*, 151, 149, 21 June 1858.
38. *The Times*, 17 September 1870, p. 5.
39. *The Times*, 4 July 1873, p. 10.
40. *Hansard*, 229, 1047, 31 May 1878.

5 Shedding daylight on the unions

1. Lowe to Henry Sherbrooke, 3 September 1867, quoted in Arthur Patchett Martin, *Life and Letters of the Right Honourable Robert Lowe, Viscount Sherbrooke*, London, 1893, vol. 2, p. 325
2. J.S. Mill, 'Thornton on Labour and its Claims, Part 2', *Fortnightly Review*, new series, 5 June 1869, pp. 680–700. The seventh and final (1871) edition of Mill's *Principles*, however, left in Mill's previous words on the wage fund, saying in its final paragraph that recent discussion on the subject was not yet ripe for incorporation in a general treatise on political economy.
3. R. Lowe, 'Trades Unions', *Quarterly Review*, 123, 1867, p. 369.
4. *The Times*, 16 January 1867, p. 8.
5. 'Trades Unions', p. 355.
6. Ibid., pp. 355–62.
7. *The Times*, 16 January 1867, p. 8.
8. Ibid.
9. 'Trades Unions', p. 356.

10. Ibid., p. 378.
11. Lowe to Gladstone, 29 August 1873, Gladstone Papers, British Library, Add. Mss. 44302, ff. 151–2.
12. Gladstone to Lowe, 3 September 1873, Gladstone Papers, Add. Mss. 44542, f. 170.
13. Memorandum by Lowe, 31 October 1873, Gladstone Papers, Add. Mss. 44621, f. 130.
14. There is a good account of these years in Jonathan Spain, 'Trade Unionists, Gladstonian Liberals, and the Labour Law Reforms of 1875' in Eugenio F. Biagini and Alastair J. Reid (eds), *Currents of Radicalism: Popular Radicalism, Organized Labour, and Party Politics in Britain, 1850–1914*, Cambridge, 1991.
15. *Parliamentary Papers*, 1877, vol. 10, 551f., Lowe's proposals were eventually implemented in the Workmen's Compensation Act of 1897.
16. *Hansard*, 3rd series, 239, 1066f., 10 April 1878.
17. *The Times*, 16 December 1872, p. 7.
18. 'Trades Unions', p. 365.

6 What shall we do for Ireland?

1. R.D. Collison Black, *Economic Thought and the Irish Question*, Cambridge, 1960, p. 31.
2. The sharpest contrast came when both Lowe and Mill used the Lakeland, the largest concentration of peasant proprietors in England, as an augury for Ireland. Whereas Mill's *Principles of Political Economy* featured a long poetic extract from Wordsworth praising their way of life, Lowe could only see 'drunken, improvident, lazy, wretched cultivators . . . very immoral and disappearing very fast . . . from their own vices . . . If these things happen on the green tree what will they do on the dry?' (Mill, *Principles*, ed. W.J. Ashley, London, 1909, p. 257n.; E.D. Steele, *Irish Land and British Politics*, Cambridge University Press, 1974, p. 93).
3. *Hansard*, 3rd series, 171, 1375, 23 June 1863 and 187, 823, 27 February 1865.
4. *Hansard*, 183, 1078, 17 May 1866.
5. *Hansard*, 183, 1081, 17 May 1866.
6. *Hansard*, 183, 1091, 17 May 1866.
7. *Hansard*, 183, 1094–5, 17 May 1866. Mill had said the same in *Principles of Political Economy*. After considering the record of, and the disincentives to, landlords in bringing about improvements, he concluded, 'Landed property in England is thus very far from completely fulfilling the conditions which render its existence economically justifiable. But if insufficiently realised even in England, in Ireland those conditions are not complied with at all. With individual exceptions (some of them very honourable ones), the owners of Irish estates do nothing for the land but drain it of its produce' (*Principles*, ed. W.J. Ashley, London, 1909, p. 232).

8. R. Lowe, 'What Shall We Do for Ireland?', *Quarterly Review*, 124, 1868, p. 271.
9. Ibid., p. 271.
10. Ibid.
11. Ibid., pp. 274–5.
12. Ibid., p. 275. Most of Lowe's contemporaries would have agreed that the small landlord was usually the worst, but not out of exceptional rapaciousness but rather because he was usually so poor himself that he was forced to force the maximum out of his tenantry. In any case, Mill was advocating that tenants be helped to purchase the land they worked themselves, not to become landlord over others. Lowe, however, as has been seen, believed that population pressure was a relentless force for subdivision, in which case his fears make sense.
13. Mill, 'England and Ireland' in J.M. Robson (ed.), *Collected Works*, Toronto, 1982, vol. 6, p. 528.
14. *Hansard*, 177, 770, 27 February 1865.
15. Lowe, 'What Shall We Do for Ireland?', pp. 273, 275.
16. Martin denies this, identifying the 1867 Reform Act as the catalyst. However, his dismissal of the Fenians rests on Lowe's words (to a friend in Australia) 'all mankind have abandoned themselves to a foolish terror of these wretched Fenians, whom I regard with great contempt...' (Arthur Patchett Martin, *Life and Letters of the Right Honourable Robert Lowe, Viscount Sherbrooke*, London, 1893, vol. 2, p. 340). Contempt for Fenianism, and for those letting it dominate their lives, is not the same as regarding it as unimportant. In Martin's own words, it was to Lowe 'a plague that must be stamped out' (Ibid., p. 345). As for the Reform Bill, Martin attributes to Lowe a justified fear that it would swamp the loyalist ascendancy with nationalist voters. It would be surprising had Lowe not had some such fears, but Martin does not show him expressing them, still less revising his views on the Irish question on their basis.
17. *Hansard*, 190, 1497, 12 March 1868.
18. *Hansard*, 190, 1489, 12 March 1868.
19. *Hansard*, 177, 771, 27 February 1865.
20. *Hansard*, 177, 773, 27 February 1865.
21. Lowe, 'What Shall We Do for Ireland?', p. 276.
22. Ibid.
23. *Hansard*, 190, 1489, 12 March 1868.
24. *The Times*, 28 January 1869, p. 7.
25. Lowe to Granville, 21 December 1869, Granville Papers, National Archive 30/29/66.
26. Lowe to Cardwell, 18 October 1869, Cardwell Papers, National Archive 30/48/22 f. 37.
27. Confidential printed memo, Lowe to Gladstone, 29 September 1869, Gladstone Papers, British Library, Add. Mss. 44611, f. 93.
28. Ibid., f. 93.
29. Lowe to Kimberley, 14 October 1869, Kimberley Papers, Bodleian Library, Ms. Eng b204. In a thorough analysis of Lowe's idea, Steele, *Irish Land and*

British Politics, convincingly argues that in the subsequent correspondence Lowe went further and 'came near to realising the tenants' desires' (p. 162). More contentiously, Steele suggests that only a lawyer like Lowe imagined the Courts could simply be shut down again once the Government pronounced them obsolete.
30. This was later amended to require the tenant's consent.
31. Lady Burghclere (ed.), *A Great Lady's Friendships: Letters to Mary, Marchioness of Salisbury and Countess of Derby, 1862–90*, London, 1933, p. 232.
32. *Hansard*, 190, 1525, 12 March 1868.
33. *Hansard*, 190, 1526, 12 March 1868.
34. *Hansard*, 190, 1525–6, 12 March 1868.
35. *Hansard*, 190, 1493, 12 March 1868.
36. Lowe, 'What Shall We Do for Ireland?', pp. 272–3.
37. J.S. Mill, 'Leslie and the Land Question' 1870, reprinted in J.M. Robson (ed.), *The Collected Works of John Stuart Mill*, Toronto, 1967, vol. 5, p. 671.
38. *Hansard*, 200, 1196–7, 4 April 1870.
39. *Hansard*, 200, 1200, 4 April 1870.
40. Treasury Papers, National Archive, T 250/7, p. 138.
41. *The Times*, 6 December 1871, p. 3.
42. *Hansard*, 210, 2027f., 30 April 1872; *Hansard*, 216, 1812, 4 July 1873. On the second occasion he conceded that prices had risen in Ireland, but invoked supply and demand as the only basis for setting wages. Better education had increased the supply of potential clerks and this, not the cost of living in Ireland, was what mattered.
43. *The Times*, 26 September 1872, p. 6 and 7 October 1872, p. 10.

7 Democratic economics or Gladstonian finance?

1. Gillian Knight, *Illiberal Liberal: Robert Lowe in New South Wales, 1842–50*, Melbourne, 1966, p. 242.
2. Speech at Edinburgh, 1 November 1867, reported in *The Times*, 4 November 1867, p. 8.
3. *Hansard*, 3rd series, 178, 1432, 3 May 1865.
4. J. Bryce, *Studies in Contemporary Biography*, London, 1903, pp. 297–8.
5. James Winter, *Robert Lowe*, Toronto, 1976, p. 202.
6. *Hansard*, 182, 151, 13 March 1866.
7. *Hansard*, 182, 155, 13 March 1866.
8. Winter, *Robert Lowe*, p. 149.
9. R. Lowe, 'Preface', *Speeches and Letters on Reform*, London, 1867, p. 8.
10. *The Times*, 8 December 1859, p. 6.
11. *The Times*, 24 April 1865, p. 8 and 26 December 1865, p. 8.
12. Lowe, 'Preface', *Speeches and Letters on Reform*, p. 7.
13. *Hansard*, 178, 1439, 3 May 1865.
14. Lowe, 'Preface', *Speeches and Letters on Reform*, p. 10.
15. Ibid., p. 149.
16. A. Howe, *Free Trade and Liberal England*, Oxford, 1997, p. 152.

17. E.F. Biagini, 'Popular Liberals, Gladstonian Finance and the Debate on Taxation, 1860–74' in Eugenio F. Biagini and Alastair J. Reid (eds), *Currents of Radicalism: Popular Radicalism, Organized Labour and Party Politics in Britain, 1850–1914*, Cambridge, 1991, p. 147.
18. R. Lowe, 'Imperialism', *Fortnightly Review*, 24, new series, 1 October 1878, p. 456.
19. Arthur Patchett Martin, *Life and Letters of the Right Honourable Robert Lowe, Viscount Sherbrooke*, London, 1893, vol. 2, p. 285.
20. R. Lowe, 'Mr Gladstone on Manhood Suffrage', *Fortnightly Review*, 22, new series, 1 December 1877, p. 740.
21. *The Times*, 23 May 1860, p. 9. Gladstone had already stated his desire that income tax payers should approximately correspond to the electorate. See Gladstone to J.L. Tabberner, 25 November 1859, quoted in H.C.G. Matthew, 'Disraeli, Gladstone and the Politics of mid-Victorian Budgets', *Historical Journal*, 22, 1979, p. 629. Matthew claims, without providing evidence, that Gladstone wanted this in order to make income tax easier to abolish.
22. *The Times*, 26 March 1860, p. 8. Writing to his brother, Lowe was even harsher: 'There is nothing more disgraceful than the Budget except the Reform Bill.' But: 'Happily the Government has undertaken to ruin our Finances and destroy our Constitution in the same year so that the one enterprise interferes with the other' (Lowe to Henry Lowe, 31 March 1860, Lowe Papers 383/18, House of Lords). Initially, however, Lowe had been rather more generous about the Budget. On 13 February 1860 he told readers of *The Times* that it was only 'at the first aspect' that the budget appeared 'so repulsive in its features that no eloquence and no advantages could secure its acceptance'. In fact Gladstone had rightly reduced tariffs well beyond the point required by the French treaty: income tax at ten pence in the pound was a fair, if repulsive, price to pay.
23. *The Times*, 27 April 1863, p. 8.
24. Ibid.
25. *The Times*, 14 October 1864, p. 7.
26. Absurd or not, it united the Liverpool Financial Reform Association with most working-class radicals (see E.F. Biagini, *Liberty, Retrenchment and Reform: Popular Liberalism in the Age of Gladstone, 1860–1880*, Cambridge, 1992, p. 110).
27. *The Times*, 15 October 1864, p. 9.
28. R. Lowe, 'The Past Session And the New Parliament', *Edinburgh Review*, 105, April 1857, p. 561.
29. *The Times*, 24 September 1860, p. 6.
30. *The Times*, 7 May 1860, p. 8. The expedients were: Changing the timing of income tax collection, and of the payment of hop duty, so that 1860/1 collected more than its share; pocketing a one-off repayment of debt by Spain; an equally one-off sale of licences to allow refreshment houses to serve wine.
31. *The Times*, 24 September 1860, p. 6.
32. *The Times*, 6 April 1861, p. 8.

33. Winter, *Robert Lowe*, p. 246.
34. '...the parts assigned by the Constitution to the Government and the House of Commons have been exactly inverted', *The Times*, 6 June 1864, p. 8.
35. Winter, *Robert Lowe*, p. 246.

8 Saying no

1. Lady Burghclere (ed.), *A Great Lady's Friendships: Letters to Mary, Marchioness of Salisbury and Countess of Derby, 1862–90*, London, 1933, p. 197. At this stage Lowe believed that minority Conservative governments were the worst, being forced to bribe any number of special interests with public money if they wanted to stay in office. Gladstone, in contrast, thought lack of a majority was an essential restraint on Disraeli's largesse. The experience of Disraeli with a majority, after 1874, soon converted Lowe to Gladstone's view.
2. James Winter, *Robert Lowe*, Toronto, 1976, p. 248.
3. Gladstone to Lowe, Gladstone Papers, British Library, Add. Mss. 44301, ff. 35–36.
4. *The Times*, 22 December 1868, p. 4.
5. *The Times*, 28 January 1869, p. 7.
6. See G.C. Peden, 'Public Expenditure, 1832–1914' in Donald Winch and Patrick K. O'Brien (eds), *The Political Economy of British Historical Experience, 1688–1914*, Oxford, 2002.
7. Hence, for instance, his letter to Gladstone in October 1869 objecting that Clarendon, the foreign secretary, had announced some spending increases 'in vague language which conveys no information correct enough for the Treasury to challenge'. Lowe to Gladstone, 27 October 1869, Gladstone Papers, British Library, Add. Mss. 44301, f. 100.
8. *The Times*, 5 September 1873, p. 3. Lowe also pressed Gladstone to have the government's accounts published weekly, citing Press and public ignorance of public finance and the prospect of a future Tory spendthrifts 'keeping us in the dark for a quarter of a year'. Lowe to Gladstone, 28 January 1870, Gladstone Papers Add. Mss. 44301, f. 120.
9. National Archive, TR 29/614, p. 314 (20 February 1869) and TR 29/613, p. 559 (29 December 1868). The index to the Treasury volume recording all this contains some thoughtful cross-referencing, for example, 'Captured Negroes – see Liberated Africans', and the present writer in his researches was delighted to read, in the Public Record Office (National Archive), of a 1869 grant by the Treasury to cover the cost of disposing of worthless papers at the Public Record Office (TR 29/615, 24 February 1869).
10. Winter, *Robert Lowe*, p. 254.
11. Lowe to Granville, 1 September 1870, Granville Papers, National Archive 30/29/66.
12. Lowe to Gladstone, 20 December 1870, Gladstone Papers, British Library, Add. Mss. 44310, f. 164.

13. *The Times*, 27 September 1872, p. 6.
14. *The Times*, 24 November 1873, p. 10.
15. Gillian Knight, *Illiberal Liberal: Robert Lowe in New South Wales, 1842–50*, Melbourne, 1966, p. 255.
16. PRO TR 29/615, p. 40, 16 April 1869.
17. Lowe to Earl Stanhope, 10 March 1873, quoted in Arthur Patchett Martin, *Life and Letters of the Right Honourable Robert Lowe, Viscount Sherbrooke*, London, 1893, vol. 2, p. 376.
18. *The Times*, 22 March 1869, p. 6.
19. Winter, *Robert Lowe*, p. 250.
20. *Hansard*, 3rd series, 211, 372, 7 May 1872. However, as Douglas Woodruff says, Lowe's remarks did nothing to abate 'the rather confused but very strong feeling that the powers that be were hounding down the Claimant because he was a poor man' (Woodruff, *The Tichborne Claimant*, London, 1957, p. 220). Woodruff also suggests (p. xiv) that Lowe's own background in Australia, whence the claimant had materialised, made him especially hostile to the claimant.
21. Because, unlike the first Tichborne hearing, it was a criminal case, depositions from witnesses were inadmissible and they had to be there in person (Woodruff, *The Tichborne Claimant*, p. 220; Lowe to Gladstone, 23 May 1872, Gladstone Papers, British Library, Add. Mss. 44302, f. 50; Gladstone to Lowe, 23 May 1872, Gladstone Papers, Add. Mss. 44531, f. 130).
22. Diary of Sir Henry Cole, 11 January 1869, quoted in D.W. Sylvester, *Robert Lowe on Education*, Cambridge, 1974, p. 210.
23. *The Times*, 28 January 1869, p. 7.
24. *The Times*, 5 September 1873, p. 3.
25. *Hansard*, 210, 763–4, 4 April 1872.
26. *Hansard*, 210, 765, 4 April 1872.
27. *Hansard*, 210, 766, 4 April 1872.
28. *Hansard*, 210, 768–9, 4 April 1872.
29. *Hansard*, 205, 1405, 20 April 1871.
30. *Hansard*, 205, 1406, 20 April 1871.
31. Lowe to Gladstone, 15 February 1873, Gladstone Papers, Add. Mss. 44302, f. 100.
32. Lowe to Gladstone, 27 May 1873, Gladstone Papers, Add. Mss. 44302, f. 125.

9 The chancellor meets his match

1. *The Times*, 3 January 1857, p. 6.
2. *Gladstone Diaries*, vol. 5 (ed. H.C.G. Matthew, Oxford, 1974), p. 197 (14 February 1857).
3. . . . and said 'Like the elephant given by some eastern prince to the man he intends to ruin, Mr Gladstone is an inmate too costly for any party to afford to keep for long.' Lowe's own party would be footing the bill

within two years. R. Lowe, 'The Past Session and the New Parliament', *Edinburgh Review*, 105, April 1857, p. 567.

4. *The Times*, 17 November 1858, p. 6. Lewis also believed that a wider range of indirect taxes would make it easier eventually to abolish income tax. See H.C.G. Matthew, 'Disraeli, Gladstone and the Politics of mid-Victorian Budgets', *Historical Journal*, 22, 1979, p. 617.
5. Gladstone was commenting on Cobden's plan for a 'National Budget', put forward in conjunction with Gladstone's future friends in the Liverpool Financial Reform Association (see Chapter 7). Cobden would have got rid of all indirect taxes, paying for this by cuts in defence and the civil list, and claiming that he could thus reduce taxes on the poor without imposing anything more on the rich. See Matthew, 'Mid-Victorian Budgets', p. 624.
6. Gladstone to Childers, 2 April 1873, printed in *Gladstone Diaries*, ed. H.C.G. Matthew, Oxford, 1982, Introduction, vol. 7, p. lxxxv. Gladstone also believed it important that those with a vote should pay income tax, to encourage them to support public economy. This is carefully argued in Matthew, 'Mid-Victorian Budgets', though the conclusion (p. 639) that 'Gladstone wanted all voters to pay income tax so as to get the tax abolished' is too bald a statement of Gladstone's position at any time in his career, let alone as a generalisation.
7. *Hansard*, 3rd series, 197, 1806, 13 July 1869.
8. *Hansard*, 194, 1532, 16 March 1869.
9. When, two years later, Lowe faced a similar motion, the Liberal MP Edward Leatham quoted his words back at him, claiming that the passage from Smith told in favour of discriminating between different sources of income. Smith had said that one should pay tax in proportion to the revenue one 'enjoys' under the protection of the state. This exempts income spent to replace capital and income spent on necessaries to keep the worker alive. Hence, while Lowe 'tells us he is taxing us in the name of Adam Smith, he is trampling that respectable economist under his feet'. Lowe retorted that when Smith wrote 'enjoy' he simply meant 'possess', and went on to repeat his remarks of 1869 almost unchanged (*Hansard*, 206, cols 1084 and 1093, 19 May 1871).
10. *The Times*, 1 April 1869, p. 8.
11. *The Times*, 9 April 1869, p. 7.
12. Much of this (corn duties, tea licences, fire insurance) was in line with a list Gladstone had sent Lowe of the things he himself would have liked to do as Chancellor but never did, though Gladstone proposed only a reduction in fire duty, not its abolition (Gladstone to Lowe, 9 January 1869, National Archive T/64/397).
13. *Hansard*, 195, 378, 8 April 1869.
14. Lowe said that he would have liked to get rid of the tax on armorial bearings altogether. 'But as I cannot get rid of it the best thing which it appears to me I can do is increase it a little.' *Hansard*, 195, 392, 8 April 1869. Why could he not get rid of it?
15. *Hansard*, 195, 374–5, 8 April 1869.

16. *The Times*, 9 April 1869, p. 7.
17. The Conservatives were still sore about this five years later: in February 1874 Lowe noted that J.G. Hubbard, seen as a possible Chancellor in a Tory government after the impending election, had said Lowe's device was 'a most wicked and abominable thing'. Let Hubbard then go back to the old way of collection, taunted Lowe. 'He will have to disgorge the £3,250,000 that I obtained from that source' (*The Times*, 4 February 1874, p. 5).
18. *Economist*, 29 May 1869, p. 622.
19. *Hansard*, 200, 1615, 11 April 1870.
20. And were soon claiming they had been proved right. In the following year's budget debate Dyce Nichol MP detailed a house in his constituency where 20 hawkers of mixed sex were huddled together, 'a state of affairs disgraceful in any county, and particularly where only a few miles distant from Her Majesty's Highland residence'. *Hansard*, 205, 1426, 20 April 1871.
21. *Hansard*, 200, 1639, 11 April 1870.
22. Ibid.
23. *The Times*, 28 January 1869, p. 7.
24. *Hansard*, 200, 1624–5, 11 April 1870. Ungraciously but characteristically, Lowe spurned the support of those who saw the tax as a stout defence of the Game Laws against poachers. 'I do not care a pin for the Game Laws. The object of the Bill is to check lawless habits. In answer to those who say it is a sign of freedom that the lower classes should go armed, I say it is the greatest proof of absence of freedom when every man goes armed' (*Hansard*, 203, 768, 22 July 1870).
25. *Hansard*, 200, 1638, 11 April 1870.
26. *Hansard*, 200, 1640, 11 April 1870.
27. *The Times*, 13 April 1870, p. 8. The previous year Lowe had told the Commons that 'I should be very glad if the House would consent to put on a 1s. income tax for the reduction of the debt; but I cannot say that I think they would allow me to do so'; which is no doubt why he felt safe in making a teasing proposal he had no intention of enacting (*Hansard*, 198, 1213, 3 August 1869).
28. *Hansard*, 200, 1620, 11 April 1870. Lowe used similar arguments the following year when resisting a proposal that £10 million be put on the estimates each year to pay off the debt. This 'cast-iron process', he said, would obstruct the recognition that 'the demands of the Revenue are greater or less in one year compared with another'. *Hansard*, 204, 1556, 7 March 1871.
29. *Hansard*, 200, 1640, 11 April 1870.
30. *Hansard*, 200, 1663, 11 April 1870.
31. *Hansard*, 200, 1670, 11 April 1870.
32. *The Times*, 28 January 1869, p. 7.
33. Quoted in James Winter, *Robert Lowe*, Toronto, 1976, p. 214.
34. Gladstone eventually came round to this view too, but not until long after France had been defeated (Gladstone to Cardwell, 9 September 1871,

National Archive 30/48/8 f. 122). Disraeli continued to insist that the destruction of the balance of power in Europe required increased spending by Britain.
35. Winter, *Robert Lowe*, p. 213.
36. *The Times*, 17 September 1870, p. 5.
37. On the lines of Switzerland, which had 'an army at very small expense equal to one-tenth of the population'. Lowe to Gladstone, 20 December 1870, Gladstone Papers, British Library, Add. Mss. 44301, f. 164.
38. Lady Burghclere (ed.), *A Great Lady's Friendships: Letters to Mary, Marchioness of Salisbury and Countess of Derby, 1862–90*, London, 1933, p. 292.
39. *Hansard*, 205, 1616, 24 April 1871.
40. Ibid.
41. *Hansard*, 205, 1647, 24 April 1871.
42. *Hansard*, 205, 1447, 20 April 1871.
43. *Hansard*, 205, 1414–15, 20 April 1871.
44. *Hansard*, 205, 1529, 20 April 1871.
45. *Hansard*, 205, 1574, 20 April 1871.
46. *The Times*, 24 April 1871, p. 12.
47. Gladstone to Lowe, Gladstone Papers, Add. Mss. 44301, ff. 35–36.
48. *The Times*, 24 April 1871, p. 12.
49. *Hansard*, 205, col. 1416, 20 April 1871.
50. E.F. Biagini (in Eugenio F. Biagini and Alastair J. Reid (eds), *Currents of Radicalism: Popular Radicalism, Organized Labour, and Party Politics in Britain, 1850–1914*, Cambridge, 1991, p. 145) suggests that Lowe chose his trio of measures in further pursuit of impartiality towards all classes (with the succession duty falling mainly on member of the upper class, the income tax increase on the middle and the match tax on the lower) and, in particular, to make sure that militarists of all stations footed the bill they had demanded be sent. Lowe himself was ambiguous on this. His speech of 18 May 1871 does suggest obliquely that the budget was designed to hit all classes equally; yet in the actual budget debate he claimed that the match tax in itself was intended as class-neutral, which would make the three measures taken as a whole class-biased (*Hansard*, 206, 984, 18 May 1871).
51. *The Times*, 25 April 1871, p. 9.
52. *The Times*, 22 April 1871, p. 9.
53. *Hansard*, 205, 1941, 27 April 1871.
54. *The Times*, 26 April 1871, p. 9.
55. *Hansard*, 205, 1409, 20 April 1871.
56. *Hansard*, 205, 1410, 20 April 1871.
57. Winter, *Robert Lowe*, p. 277.
58. *Hansard*, 208, 1729, 15 August 1871.
59. *Hansard*, 206, 1456, 2 June 1871.
60. Lowe, confidential printed memo. 'Consolidated Debt and Quarterly Payment of Dividends', 28 February 1870, Gladstone Papers, Add. Mss. 44613, f. 172.
61. *Hansard*, 210, 629, 25 March 1872.

62. Matthew, 'Disraeli, Gladstone and the Politics of mid-Victorian Budgets', p. 616.
63. *Hansard*, 225, 1051, 28 April 1873.
64. *Hansard*, 225, 1049, 28 April 1873.
65. *Hansard*, 225, 1052, 28 April 1873.
66. *Hansard*, 225, 1053, 28 April 1873.
67. Nor was it even possible to be very accurate as to how inaccurate it was. Taxpayers made a separate return under each schedule of income tax, and no return of total income. There are thus no official figures of how many were in each income bracket at any given time (see Matthew, 'Disraeli, Gladstone and the Politics of mid-Victorian Budgets', pp. 628f. for further discussion of this).
68. See Biagini and Reid, *Currents of Radicalism*, pp. 148–9. Unbeknown to Lowe, Gladstone was already toying with the abolition of income tax, a measure he was to bring forward on replacing Lowe as Chancellor later that year, but failed to enact because he lost office before he could bring in a budget (see Gladstone to H.C.E. Childers, 2 April 1873, Gladstone Papers, Add. Mss. 44613, f. 105). Gladstone realised that indirect taxation could not make up all the resulting gap in the revenue, but sounds ambiguous as to whether it should make up any of it. He also received a deputation from the Anti-Income Tax League a few days after Lowe's budget and told them that his 'own desires were in the same direction' as theirs (*Gladstone Diairies*, ed. H.C.G. Matthew, Oxford, 1982, vol. 8, p. 319n.)
69. *Hansard*, 200, 1629–30, 11 April 1870. See also *Hansard*, 215, 709, 7 April 1873.
70. *Hansard*, 200, col. 709, 7 April 1873.
71. *Hansard*, 197, 1806, 13 July 1869.
72. The year 1873 was bad for Lowe in every respect. His vicissitudes included a court appearance when he refused to pay his butler *in lieu* of notice. The butler had been dismissed for sitting down in Mrs Lowe's drawing room. However the judge upheld Lowe's action, ruling that, had the butler sat down to tie up his shoelace, dismissal would have been too harsh a penalty. Sitting down because he 'felt tired', however, was, on the mature deliberation of the Bench, impertinence of an order of reprehensibility sufficient to warrant instant sacking. *The Times*, 6 May 1873, p. 9 and 7 May 1873, p. 12.
73. *Hansard*, 216, cols 686–711, 9 June 1873.
74. *Gladstone Diaries*, 2 August 1873, vol. 8, p. 364.
75. Until 1919, MPs who became ministers had to resign their seats and fight a by-election. Lowe told Gladstone that this applied equally to MPs picking up a second portfolio concurrently with their first, but legal opinion disagreed with him.
76. W. Bagehot, 'Mr Lowe as Chancellor of the Exchequer' in R.H. Hutton (ed.), *Biographical Studies*, London, 1881, p. 351.
77. Ibid., pp. 351–2.

78. Lowe to Derby, letter dated 'Home Office, 1873', quoted in Arthur Patchett Martin, *Life and Letters of the Right Honourable Robert Lowe, Viscount Sherbrooke*, London, 1893, vol. 2, p. 463.
79. Gladstone to Lowe, 13 August 1873, Gladstone Papers, Add. Mss. 44302, f. 144.
80. Ibid., f. 144.
81. *The Times*, 5 September 1873, p. 3.
82. *The Times*, 6 September 1873, p. 6.
83. Gladstone to Granville, 9 September 1873, quoted in John Morley, *Life of Gladstone*, London, 1903, vol. 1, p. 1010.
84. *The Times*, 4 July 1873, p. 10.
85. *The Times*, 5 September 1873, p. 3.
86. *The Times*, 24 November 1873, p. 10.
87. 'The enormous surpluses of the later years of the government were the result of buoyant economic conditions rather than fierce retrenchment.' J. Parry, 'Gladstone, Liberalism and the Government of 1868–74' in D. Bebbington and R. Swift (eds), *Gladstone Centenary Essays*, Liverpool, 2000, p. 102.
88. S. Buxton, *Finance and Politics*, London, 1888, vol. 2, p. 156.
89. Gladstone to Lowe, 30 August 1871, Gladstone Papers, Add. Mss. 44540, f. 98.
90. *Gladstone Diaries*, 14 December 1871, vol. 8, p. 77.
91. Gladstone to Lowe, 29 January 1872, reprinted in *Gladstone Diaries*, vol. 8, p. 103.
92. Gladstone to Goschen, 9 November 1872, Gladstone Papers, Add. Mss. 44542, f. 41.
93. Most recently in K. Theodore Hoppen, *The mid-Victorian Generation, 1846–1886*, Oxford, 1998, p. 606.
94. B. Mitchell and P. Deane, *Abstract of British Historical Statistics*, Cambridge, 1988. This is comparing the last (and only) fiscal year with a Hunt budget (1868/9) to the last fiscal year with a Lowe budget (1873/4). The raw figures show even larger drops in spending but certain items were excluded from Army and Navy headings after 1869, and I have followed Mitchell and Deane in their estimate (p. 595) that this made a difference of 10 per cent to the Army and 5 per cent to the Navy figures. Note also that the 1868/9 figures exclude the cost of the Abyssinian expedition while those for 1873/4 do not exclude the cost of the Ashanti war. To this extent even these figures are unfair to Lowe and too kind to his critics.
95. *Gladstone Diaries*, ed. M.R.D. Foot & H.C.G. Mathew, 14 vols, Oxford, Clarendon Press, 1968–94, vol. 7 (1982), introduction, pp. lxxxix–xc.
96. See W.N. Calkins, 'A Victorian Free Trade Lobby: The Liverpool Financial Reform Association, 1848–1914', *Economic History Review*, 13, 2nd series, 1960, pp. 90–104.
97. Mitchell and Deane, *Abstract of British Historical Statistics*.
98. Martin, *Life and Letters*, vol. 2, p. 371.

10 Joining the 'Europe' and shrinking the pound

1. L. Einaudi, 'From the franc to the "Europe": The Attempted Transformation of the Latin Monetary Union into a European Monetary Union, 1865–1873', *Economic History Review*, 53, 2000, p. 286.
2. Report of Royal Commission on International Coinage, *Parliamentary Papers*, 1867–8, XXVII, p. 13.
3. Bagehot later proposed an Anglo-American monetary union which he believed Germany would want to join too, but the idea attracted very little support anywhere.
4. Report of Royal Commission, p. 128.
5. Ibid., p. 134.
6. Ibid., p. 16.
7. Ibid., p. 14.
8. Ibid., p. 23.
9. D.P. O'Brien (ed.), *The Correspondence of Lord Overstone*, Cambridge, 1971, vol. 3, pp. 1140–6.
10. W.S. Jevons, 'On the Condition of the Metallic Currency of the United Kingdom, with reference to the Question of International Coinage', *Journal of the Statistical Society of London*, 31, 1868, p. 431.
11. Ibid., p. 430.
12. *Correspondence of Lord Overstone*, vol. 3, p. 1179.
13. Ibid., p. 1180. It was one of Overstone's objections to Jevons that he used 'mintage' (the cost of coining) and 'seignorage' (any profit above this) interchangeably.
14. However, critics were quick to point out that Jevons only got a sufficient mintage charge to cover the shrinkage of the pound by having the combined charge for mintage and remintage (of worn coins) fall on mintage alone. Where was the justice in that? (see for instance 'H.M.H.', 'The Gold Coinage', letter to *The Daily Telegraph*, 9 October 1869).
15. Printed confidential memo, 'Necessity for Imposing a charge upon the Coinage of Gold Bullion at the Royal Mint', 2 June 1869, Gladstone Papers, British Library, Add. Mss. 44610, f. 83.
16. Einaudi, 'From the franc to the "Europe"', p. 299.
17. *Hansard*, 3rd series, 198, 1408–9, 6 August 1869.
18. *Hansard*, 198, 1421, 6 August 1869.
19. *Hansard*, 198, 1533, 10 August 1869.
20. *The Times*, 9 August 1869.
21. *Hansard*, 198, 1533, 10 August 1869.
22. *Morning Advertiser*, 14 August 1869. It was almost inevitable that someone would propose calling the new coin the 'Lowe', and now someone did (letter to *The Times* by 'Par', 13 September 1869).
23. Lowe to Cardwell, 7 September 1869, Gladstone Papers, Add. Mss. 44611, f. 54.
24. Cardwell to Gladstone, 19 September 1869, Gladstone Papers, Add. Mss. 44119, f. 66.

25. Gladstone to Cardwell, 20 September 1869, Gladstone Papers, Add. Mss. 44537, f. 66.
26. Lowe's next letter to Gladstone was to request the abolition of the post of Master of the Mint, to save money. It is unclear why Einaudi sees Gladstone's reply, which is entirely about the affairs of the Mint, as an order to Lowe to 'calm down' on the European currency; though Gladstone's scrawl, which has caused Einaudi to read 'establishment' as 'sovereign's weight', is not helpful (Lowe to Gladstone, 11 October 1869, Gladstone Papers, Add. Mss. 44301, ff. 84–5; Gladstone to Lowe, 12 October 1869, ibid., Add. Mss. 44537, f. 92v; Einaudi, 'From the franc to the "Europe"', p. 299).
27. *Hansard*, 199, 153, 10 February 1870. The Banque de France remained solidly in favour of bimetallism, the Senate voted against a gold standard and the French government itself was split on the subject. See Einaudi, 'From the franc to the "Europe"', passim.
28. *Hansard*, 201, 333, 15 July 1870.
29. *Hansard*, 197, 471f., 23 June 1869.
30. *Hansard*, 197, 484, 23 June 1869.
31. See p. 131, Chapter 11. A gold-exchange standard is where gold coins do not circulate but the paper currency is fully backed by gold.
32. *Hansard*, 212, 1290, 16 July 1872.
33. Ibid.
34. Lowe to Gladstone *et al.*, confidential printed memo. 'Paper Money', 20 November 1870, Gladstone Papers, Add. Mss. 44619, f. 107.
35. Lowe to Gladstone, 26 December 1870, Gladstone Papers, Add. Mss. 44301, f. 170.
36. Gladstone to Lowe, 31 March 1871, Gladstone Papers, Add. Mss. 44301, f. 187.
37. Lowe to Gladstone, 27 March 1873, Gladstone Papers, Add. Mss. 44302, f. 121.
38. *Hansard*, 225, 123, 25 March 1873.
39. *Hansard*, 225, 147–50, 25 March 1873.

11 Beer, bankruptcy and empire

1. R. Lowe 'Have We Abolished Imprisonment for Debt?', *Fortnightly Review*, 21, new series, 1 March 1877, p. 313.
2. Ibid.
3. R. Lowe, 'The Birmingham Plan of Public House Reform', *Fortnightly Review*, vol. 21, new series, 1 January 1877, p. 4.
4. Ibid., p. 5.
5. Ibid., pp. 6–7. In a follow-up letter to *The Times*, Lowe pointed out that Chamberlain himself had recently argued that drunkenness had nothing to do with the density of pubs, and cited convincing figures to prove it. *The Times*, 23 January 1877, p. 5.
6. R. Lowe, 'The Value to the United Kingdom of the Foreign Dominions', *Fortnightly Review*, 23, new series, 1 November 1877, p. 620.

7. Ibid.
8. *The Times*, 11 October 1859, p. 6.
9. *The Times*, 24 July 1863, p. 8.
10. Early on in his Chancellorship Lowe had become involved in an ill-tempered argument about how much booty a particular division of English soldiers might retain from their part in suppressing the Mutiny (such cases were by tradition heard by the Treasury). See *Hansard*, 3rd series, 201, 1527f., 27 May 1870.
11. 'The Value to the United Kingdom of the Foreign Dominions', pp. 624–5.
12. R. Lowe, 'A Simple Way Out of the Indian Difficulty', *Fortnightly Review*, vol. 36, new series, 1 July 1879, p. 24.
13. R. Lowe, 'Imperialism', *Fortnightly Review*, vol. 24, new series, 1 October 1878, p. 454.
14. Ibid.
15. Ibid., p. 456.
16. Ibid., p. 457.
17. Ibid., p. 458.
18. *The Times*, 5 April 1860, p. 8.
19. 'A Simple Way Out of the Indian Difficulty', p. 28.
20. Lowe made the same proposal in parliament in 1879, suggesting that what was good for India would be equally good for Britain, but accepting that 'English prejudices would not hear of [a gold exchange standard] for a moment'. *Hansard*, 246, 1189, 23 May 1879.
21. 'A Simple Way Out of the Indian Difficulty', p. 36.
22. R. Lowe, 'What is Money?', *Nineteenth Century*, 11 April 1882, pp. 505–6.
23. Ibid., p. 504.
24. Ibid., p. 509.

12 Pig philosophy?

1. Gladstone's 'contamination of the truths of financial science' comes from *The Times*, 27 February 1860, p. 6. All other remarks quoted in this paragraph have already appeared in this book.
2. R. Lowe, 'Recent Attacks on Political Economy', *Nineteenth Century*, 4, 1878, p. 865.
3. Ibid., p. 866.
4. Ibid. Cliffe Leslie rightly found this concession of Lowe's inadequate pointing out that Chapter 1 of *The Wealth of Nations*, 'bears all the marks of wide research and induction'. Of course Smith did not set before the reader every historical and statistical fact he had discovered. 'A discoverer would be avoided like the pestilence if he did this' and no doubt this kind of thing was in the papers Smith had burnt shortly before he died (T.E.C. Leslie, 'Political Economy and Sociology' (1879), reprinted in *Essays in Political Economy* (2nd edition, London, 1888, p. 206).
5. 'Recent Attacks on Political Economy', p. 867.
6. Political Economy Club, *Revised report at the proceedings at the Dinner of 31st May, 1876*, London, 1876, pp. 7–8.

7. 'Recent Attacks on Political Economy', p. 864.
8. Ibid., p. 868. G.C.G. Moore comments, 'I contend that these admissions were no more than cosmetic qualifications designed to meet the numerous criticisms of his approach.' Taken purely in the context of 'Recent Attacks on Political Economy' this is an arguable position. (Though even here one might comment that falsifying his beliefs was not exactly a *leitmotif* of Lowe's, and, if he is not being accused of this, what exactly is 'cosmetic' about his remarks?) But the testimony of Lowe's earlier writings in *The Times* shows his lifelong awareness that the conditions of application had to be right for political economy to make headway (G.C.G. Moore, 'Robert Lowe and the Role of the Vulgar Economist in the English Methodenstreit', *Journal of Economic Methodology*, 3, 1996, p. 86).
9. This, as Cliffe Leslie was to point out, was essentially the same as Bagehot's position, though Bagehot went further than Lowe and limited political economy to 'England at its present state of commercial development and to the male sex in England' (Leslie, 'Political Economy and Sociology', p. 207). Leslie said that this, if accepted, proved on its own that political economy began with induction – the induction needed to decide which societies were ripe for the political economy treatment. Bagehot agreed with this last point, and there is no reason to think Lowe would have objected either. It was, in fact, a common position in late nineteenth-century political economy, and Sir Henry Maine, whose study of comparative law did so much to advance this attitude in the work of others, held it strongly himself (see for instance 'The Effects of Observation of India on Modern European Thought', his Rede Lecture at Cambridge University, 1875, reprinted in Maine, 1876).
10. Political Economy Club, *Proceedings of 31st May 1876*, pp. 14–19.
11. 'Recent Attacks on Political Economy', p. 864.
12. *The Times*, 2 October 1865, p. 9.
13. 'Recent Attacks on Political Economy', p. 860.
14. Ibid., pp. 861–2.
15. Ibid., p. 868.
16. Leslie, 'Political Economy and Sociology', p. 203.
17. Ibid., p. 198.
18. Ibid.
19. Ibid., p. 202.
20. Ibid., p. 211.
21. Ibid., p. 210.
22. Ibid., p. 212.
23. Ibid., p. 219.
24. Moore, 'Robert Lowe and the Role of the Vulgar Economist', p. 85.

13 Vapulo, veneo, exulo, fio

1. Lowe to A.C. Tupp, 11 June 1880, Bodleian Library, Ms. Eng. Lett. d148.
2. Lowe to Tupp, 28 September 1881, quoted in Arthur Patchett Martin, *Life and Letters of the Right Honourable Robert Lowe, Viscount Sherbrooke*, London, 1893, vol. 2, p. 458.

3. R. Lowe, 'A New Reform Bill', *Fortnightly Review*, 22, new series, 1877, quoted in Martin, *Life and Letters*, vol. 2, p. 445. 'Happier words', commented Matthew Arnold (not always a Lowe enthusiast), 'could not well be found: such is, indeed, the ideal of the Liberal Party' (Ibid., p. 445).
4. 'Newspaper comments on a late accident on the Solent', Lowe Papers, House of Lords, 383/105.

Select Bibliography

Manuscript sources

Cardwell Papers, National Archive.
Clarendon Papers, Bodleian Library.
Delane Papers, News International Archives.
Gladstone Papers, British Library.
Granville Papers, National Archive.
Kimberley Papers, Bodleian Library.
Lowe Papers, House of Lords.
Ripon Papers, British Library.
Treasury Papers, National Archive.

Official papers

Hansard's Parliamentary Debates.
Parliamentary Papers.

Newspapers and journals

The Daily Telegraph.
Economist.
Morning Advertiser.
Pall Mall Gazette.
Spectator.
The Times.

Printed sources (primary)

Arnold, Matthew, 'Culture and Anarchy' in R.H. Super (ed.), *The Complete Prose Works of Matthew Arnold*, Ann Arbor, University of Michigan Press, 1965.

——, 'The Twice Revised Code', *Fraser's Magazine*, March 1862, 347–65.

Bagehot, W., 'Mr Lowe as Chancellor of the Exchequer' (1st publ. 1871), reprinted in *Biographical Studies*, London, Longmans, Green, 1881, 350–4.

Bryce, J., *Studies in Contemporary Biography*, London, Macmillan, 1903.

Burghclere, Lady, *A Great Lady's Friendships: Letters to Mary, Marchioness of Salisbury and Countess of Derby, 1862–90*, London, Macmillan, 1933.

Buxton, S., *Finance and Politics*, 2 vols, London, J. Murray, 1888.

——, *Mr Gladstone as Chancellor of the Exchequer*, London, John Murray, 1901.
Cairnes, J.E., 'Political Economy and Laissez-Faire', reprinted in *Essays in Political Economy: Theoretical and Applied*, London, Macmillan, 1873.
Calkins, W.N., 'A Victorian Free Trade Lobby: The Liverpool Financial Reform Association, 1848–1914', *Economic History Review*, 13, 2nd series, 1960, 90–104.
Cole, Sir Henry, *Fifty Years of Public Work*, London, George Bell, 1884.
Crawford, R.W., *Speeches, Letters, Articles & c. on the Gold Coinage Controversy of 1869*, printed for private circulation by the Bank of England, 1870.
Dunham, A.L., *The Anglo-French Treaty of Commerce of 1860*, Norwood, University of Michigan Press, 1930.
[Gilbert, W.S.], 'F. Latour Tomline and Gilbert A'Beckett', *The Happy Land*, London, Last, 1873.
Gladstone, W.E., 'The County Franchise and Mr Lowe Thereon', *Nineteenth Century*, 2, November 1877, 537–60.
——, 'Last Words on the County Franchise', *Nineteenth Century*, 3, January 1878, 196–208.
Gladstone Diaries, ed. M.R.D. Foot and H.C.G. Matthew, 14 vols, Oxford, Clarendon Press, 1968–94.
Hamilton, Lord George, *Parliamentary Reminiscences and Reflections, 1868–85*, London, John Murray, 1916.
Hodgson, Geoffrey, *How Economics Forget History*, London, Routledge, 2001.
Hogan, James, *Robert Lowe: Viscount Sherbrooke*, London, Ward & Downey, 1893.
Ingram, J.K., 'The Present Position of Political Economy' (1878), reprinted in R.L. Smyth (ed.), *Essays in Economic Method*, London, Duckworth, 1962.
Jevons, W.S., *The Match Tax: A Problem in Finance*, London, E. Stanford, 1871.
Keynes, J.N., *The Scope and Method of Political Economy*, London, Macmillan, 1890.
Leslie, T.E. Cliffe, 'Political Economy and Sociology' (1879), reprinted in *Essays in Political Economy* (2nd edn), London, Longmans, 1888.
Lowe, R., 'The Past Session and the New Parliament', *Edinburgh Review*, 105, 1857, 552–78.
——, 'Mr Gladstone's Financial Statements', *Home and Foreign Review*, January 1864, 1–18.
——, *Primary and Classical Education, An Address Delivered Before the Philosophical Institution of Edinburgh*, Edinburgh, Edmonton & Douglas 1867.
——, *Speeches and Letters on Reform*, London, Bush, 1867.
——, 'Trades Unions', *Quarterly Review*, 123, 1867, 355–85.
——, *Middle Class and Primary Education, Two Speeches by the Rt. Hon. Robert Lowe, MP*, Liverpool, Robert John Bush 1868.
——, 'What Shall We Do for Ireland?', *Quarterly Review*, 124, 1868, 255–86.
——, 'Shall We Create a New University?', *Fortnightly Review*, 21, new series, 1877, 160–71.
——, 'A New Reform Bill', *Fortnightly Review*, 22, new series, 1877, 437–52.
——, 'The Birmingham Plan of Public House Reform', *Fortnightly Review*, vol. 21, new series, 1 January 1877, 1–9.

——, 'Have We Abolished Imprisonment for Debt?', *Fortnightly Review*, 21, new series, 1 March 1877, 307–16.
——, 'The Value to the United Kingdom of the Foreign Dominions', *Fortnightly Review*, 23, new series, 1 November 1877, 618–30.
——, 'Mr Gladstone on Manhood Suffrage', *Fortnightly Review*, 22, new series, 1 December 1877, 733–46.
——, 'Imperialism', *Fortnightly Review*, 24, new series, 1878, 453–65.
——, 'Recent Attacks on Political Economy', *Nineteenth Century*, 4, 1878, 858–68.
——, 'Reciprocity and Free Trade', *Nineteenth Century*, 5, 1879, 992–1002.
——, 'A Simple Way Out of the Indian Difficulty', *Fortnightly Review*, 26, new series, 1 July 1879, 24–37.
——, 'Legislation for Ireland', *Nineteenth Century*, 8, November 1880, 677–89.
——, 'What Shall We Do with Our Bankrupts?', *Nineteenth Century*, 10, 1881, 308–16.
——, 'What is Money?', *Nineteenth Century*, 11 April 1882, 501–9.
——, *Poems of a Life*, London, Kegan Paul, Trench, 1885.
Maine, Henry, *Village Communities in the East and West*, London, Murray, 1876.
Martin, Arthur Patchett, *Life and Letters of the Right Honourable Robert Lowe, Viscount Sherbrooke*, 2 vols, London, Longmans, 1893.
Mill, J.S., *A System of Logic*, 2 vols, London, Parker, 1843.
——, *Essays on Some Unsettled Questions of Political Economy*, London, John W. Parker, 1844.
——, Parliamentary speech on Irish Land Reform, 12 March 1868.
——, 'Leslie and the Land Question' (1870), reprinted in J.M. Robson (ed.), *The Collected Works of John Stuart Mill*, vol. 5, Toronto, University of Toronto Press, 1967.
——, *Principles of Political Economy*, variorum edition in J.M. Robson (ed.), *The Collected Works of John Stuart Mill*, vol. 3, Toronto, University of Toronto Press, 1967.
——, *England and Ireland* (1868), reprinted in J.M. Robson (ed.), *The Collected Works of John Stuart Mill*, vol. 5, Toronto, University of Toronto Press, 1982.
Morley, J., *The Life of William Ewart Gladstone*, 3 vols, London, Macmillan, 1903.
——, *The Life of Richard Cobden*, London, T. Fisher Unwin, 1910.
Northcote, Stafford, *Twenty Years of Financial Policy*, London, Saunders, 1862.
O'Brien, D.P. (ed.), *The Correspondence of Lord Overstone*, 3 vols, Cambridge, Cambridge University Press, 1971.
Political Economy Club, *Revised Report at the Proceedings at the Dinner of 31st May, 1876*, London, 1876.
Ricardo, D., *Principles of Political Economy* (1st publ. 1815), ed. P. Sraffa, Cambridge, Cambridge University Press, 1951.
The Sheffield outrages: Report Presented to the Trades Unions Commissioners in 1867 (1st edn), reprinted with an introduction by Sidney Pollard, Bath, Adams and Dart for Social Documents Ltd, 1971.

Smith, Adam, *The Wealth of Nations* (1st publ. 1776), 2 vols, Oxford, Clarendon Press, 1976.

Torrens, Robert, *A Letter to Nassau William Senior, Esq.: In Reply to the Article Free Trade and Retaliation in the Edinburgh Review No. CLVII*, London, Smith, Elder, 1843.

Printed sources (secondary)

Baysinger, B. and Tollison, R., 'Chaining Leviathan: The Case of Gladstonian Finance', *History of Political Economy*, 12, 1980, 206–13.

Biagini, E.F., 'British Trade Unions and Popular Political Economy, 1860–80', *Historical Journal*, 30, 4, 1987, 811–40.

——, *Liberty, Retrenchment and Reform: Popular Liberalism in the Age of Gladstone, 1860–1880*, Cambridge, Cambridge University Press, 1992.

Biagini, E.F. and Reid, A.J. (eds), *Currents of Radicalism: Popular Radicalism, Organized Labour and Party Politics in Britain, 1850–1914*, Cambridge, Cambridge University Press, 1991.

Black, R.D. Collison, *Economic Thought and the Irish Question*, Cambridge, Cambridge University Press, 1960.

——, 'The Political Economy of Thomas Edward Cliffe Leslie (1826–82): A Re-assessment', *European Journal of the History of Economic Thought*, 9, 2002, 17–41.

Blaug, M., 'The Economics of Education in English Classical Political Economy' in A. Skinner and T. Wilson (eds), *Essays on Adam Smith*, Oxford, Clarendon Press, 1975.

——, *Economic Theory in Retrospect* (5th edn), Cambridge, Cambridge University Press, 1996.

Briggs, Asa, *Victorian People*, London, Odhams, 1954.

Brown, Lucy, *The Board of Trade and the Free Trade Movement*, Oxford, Clarendon Press, 1958.

Clements, J., 'British Trade Unions and Popular Political Economy, 1850–75', *Economic History Review*, 14, 2nd series, 1961, 93–104.

Coats, A.W. (ed.), *The Classical Economists and Economic Policy*, London, Methuen, 1971.

Commercial Diplomacy, 1860–1902, printed for private circulation by the Foreign Office, 1902.

Corry, B.A., *Money, Saving and Investment in English Economics 1800 to 1850*, London, Macmillan, 1962.

Cowling, M., *1867, Disraeli, Gladstone and Revolution*, Cambridge, Cambridge University Press, 1967.

Duke, Christopher, 'Robert Lowe: A Reappraisal', *British Journal of Educational Studies*, 14, 1965, 19–35.

Dunbabin, J.P.D., 'The Revolt of the Field: The Agricultural Labourers' Movement of the 1870s', *Past and Present*, 26, November 1963, 68–97.

Dunham, A.L., *The Anglo-French Treaty of Commerce of 1860*, Norwood, University of Michigan Press, 1930.

Einaudi, L., 'From the Franc to the "Europe": The Attempted Transformation of the Latin Monetary Union into a European Monetary Union, 1865–1873', *Economic History Review*, 53, 2, 2000.

——, *Politics and Money*, Oxford, Oxford University Press, 2001.

Gosden, P.H.J.H., *The Friendly Societies in England: 1815–1875*, Manchester, Manchester University Press, 1961.

Hilton, A. Boyd, *The Age of Atonement*, Cambridge, Cambridge University Press, 1988.

Hirst, F.W., *Gladstone as Financier and Economist*, London, Ernest Benn, 1931.

History of the Times, 4 vols, 1936–9, London, *The Times*.

Hoppen, K.T., *The mid-Victorian Generation, 1846–1886*, Oxford, Clarendon Press, 1998.

Howe, Anthony, *Free Trade and Liberal England 1846–1946*, Oxford, Oxford University Press, 1997.

Iliasu, A., 'The Role of Free Trade Treaties in British Foreign Policy, 1859–1871', Ph.D. thesis, University of London, 1965.

Irwin, Douglas A., *Against the Tide: An Intellectual History of Free Trade*, Princeton, Princeton University Press, 1996.

Jenkins, R.H., *Gladstone*, London, Macmillan, 1995.

Knight, Gillian, *Illiberal Liberal: Robert Lowe in New South Wales, 1842–50*, Melbourne, Melbourne University Press, 1966.

Koot, G.M., 'T.E. Cliffe Leslie, Irish Social Reformer, and the Origins of the English Historical School of Economics', *History of Political Economy*, Fall 1975.

Marsh, Peter, *Bargaining on Europe: Britain and the First Common Market, 1860–1892*, New Haven, CT and London, Yale University Press, 1999.

Matthew, H.C.G., 'Disraeli, Gladstone and the Politics of mid-Victorian Budgets', *Historical Journal*, 22, 1979, 615–43.

——, *Gladstone*, vol. 2, Oxford, Clarendon Press, 1995.

McCredy, J., 'The British Labour Lobby', *Canadian Journal of Economics*, 22, 1956, 141–60.

Mitchell, B. and Deane, P., *Abstract of British Historical Statistics*, Cambridge University Press, 1962.

Moore, G.C.G., 'Robert Lowe and the Role of the Vulgar Economist in the English Methodenstreit', *Journal of Economic Methodology*, 3, December 1996, 69–90.

O'Brien, D.P., *The Classical Political economists*, Oxford, Clarendon Press, 1975.

Parry, J., *Democracy and Religion: Gladstone and the Liberal Party 1867–1885*, Cambridge, Cambridge University Press, 1986.

——, *The Rise and Fall of Liberal Government in Victorian Britain*, New Haven, Yale University Press, 1993.

Redish, A., 'The Latin Monetary Union and the Emergence of the International Gold Standard', in M.D. Bordo and F. Capie (eds), *Monetary Regimes in Transition*, Cambridge, Cambridge University Press, 1993.

Robbins, L., *Robert Torrens and the Evolution of Classical Economics*, London, Macmillan, 1958.

Saville, J. (ed.), *Democracy and the Labour Movement*, London, Lawrence & Wishart, 1954.

Shannon, R., *Gladstone*, 2 vols, London, Hamilton, 1982 and London, Allen Lane, 1999.

Steele, E.D., *Irish Land and British Politics*, Cambridge University Press, 1974.

——, *Palmerston and Liberalism*, Cambridge, Cambridge University Press, 1991.

Sylvester, D.W., *Robert Lowe on Education*, Cambridge, Cambridge University Press, 1974.

Taylor, A.J., *State and Laissez-Faire and State Intervention in Nineteenth-Century Britain*, London, Macmillan, 1972.

Vint, J., *Capital and Wages: A Lakatosian History of the Wage Fund Doctrine*, Aldershot, Edward Elgar, 1994.

Webb, S. and Webb, B., *The History of Trades Unionism*, London, Longmans, 1920.

West, E.G., Public versus Private Education, *Journal of Political Economy*, 72, October 1964, 465–75.

Wilson, Ted, *Battles for the Standard*, Aldershot, Ashgate, 2000.

Winch, Donald and Patrick K. O'Brien, *The Political Economy of British Historical Experience, 1688–1914*, Oxford, Oxford University Press, 2002.

Winter, James, *Robert Lowe*, Toronto, University of Toronto Press, 1976.

Woodruff, D., *The Tichborne Claimant: A Victorian Mystery*, London, Hollis & Carter, 1957.

Index